PURIM

— AND THE —

Persian Empire

A Historical, Archaeological, & Geographical Perspective

YEHUDA LANDY

FELDHEIM PUBLISHERS
JERUSALEM · NEW YORK

The integrated translation of Megillas Esther is taken from

THE MARGOLIN EDITION OF THE TORAH
CHUMASH WITH HAFTAROS, THE FIVE MEGILLOS,
AND THE COMPLETE SABBATH PRAYERS

translated by Rabbi Binyamin S. Moore

First published 2010
Copyright © 2010 by Rabbi Yehuda Landy (nzion@smile.net.il), except
for photographs otherwise noted

ISBN 978-1-59826-519-4

FELDHEIM PUBLISHERS
POB 43163/Jerusalem, Israel

208 Airport Executive Park
Nanuet, NY 10954

www.feldheim.com

10 9 8 7 6 5 4 3 2 1

Printed in Israel

Contents

לע"נ

אברהם מתתיהו ב"ר יואל פוס ע"ה

נלב"ע ב' אלול תשס"ט

Dedicated to the memory of

Abraham M. Fuss

who passed away having led a full life

❖ of Torah learning and scholarly writing

❖ of a deep love of books

❖ of a constant interest in Jewish history and law

❖ of rare accomplishment for Am Yisrael,
having founded the Haredi Center for Technological Studies,
which paved the way for thousands of Haredi families
to earn their livelihood with honor.

He will be sorely missed.

ב"ה

19 Tevet 5770
5 January 2010

Rabbi Yehuda Landy has written a brilliant book "Purim and the Persian Empire." The book combines enormous Talmudic, historical, and archeological scholarship of the highest order with illuminating illustrations and great readability. All of us who are fascinated by the story and holiday of Purim but do not quite know how to put the pieces together in the context of Jewish and general history will find their answer to this problem in this work. Rabbi Landy is a noted scholar, lecturer and author and this work is a testimony to his erudition and communicative skills. This is a don't miss book for scholar and novice alike.

With all blessings, I remain,

Rabbi Berel Wein
Rav Beit Knesset HaNassi Jerusalem
Director, Destiny Foundation

Rabbi Berel Wein
Director

United States Office:
386 Route 59
Monsey, NY 10952
845-368-1425
845-368-1528 fax
800-499-9346
info@jewishdestiny.com
www.RabbiWein.com

Israel Office:
P.O. Box 23671
Jerusalem, Israel 91236
011-972-58-339-560
011-972-2-586-8536 fax
scubac@netvision.net.il

THE DESTINY FOUNDATION

Foreword

I'M OFTEN ASKED HOW I GOT INVOLVED SO HEAVILY WITH the geography and archaeology of the Tanach. This is not an easy question for me to answer. The subject has fascinated me from a young age.

Besides my *limudei kodesh*, I have been familiarizing myself with the geography, history, and archaeology of Eretz Yisrael for many years. These topics helped me look at the Tanach and Mishnah from a different perspective. Yet the area and time period of Megillas Esther were beyond my scope of research. Having no direct access to Iran or to the ancient artifacts therein limited my ability to really study this material in depth.

That all changed when I visited a special exhibition at the British Museum in London about four years ago. The exhibition, named "Forgotten Empire," dealt exclusively with the material culture from the same Persian Empire with which we are familiar from the Megillah. This exhibition featured artifacts from Shushan normally on display at the Louvre Museum in Paris as well as artifacts which were loaned by the museums of Iran. Some of these had never been let out of the country before and because of their value are rarely on display in Iran itself.

The exhibition portrayed the glory, power, and administration of the Persian Empire, which is not easy to describe in words. I remember viewing the section "The Royal Table," which showed gold and silver tableware from the days of the empire. The setup portrayed a vivid idea of what the banquet might have looked like in the days of the Megillah. The scene was overwhelming. It was mind-boggling to imagine that in the days of Achashverosh, there were so many of these vessels that none was ever used twice. Unfortunately, the dim lighting at the exhibition did not enable the museum to properly photo-graph this section, and thus no pictures are available. The museum, however, kindly supplied me with a photo of their exquisite collection of tableware from the days of the empire. This photo can be seen on page 55.

Despite my brief stay in London, I visited the exhibition numerous times, each time discovering more artifacts that helped visualize the story of the Megillah.

The exhibition ended a short time later, but the catalogue accompanying it enabled me to understand the material more in depth. When I read the Megillah on the following Purim I was able to visualize many of the items and places mentioned there.

In our days, using archaeological evidence in the *beis midrash* is shunned. There are two main reasons for this. First, the impression in the Torah world is that archaeology is synonymous with denying the authenticity of the Tanach. Others feel that there is no need to bring archaeology into the *beis midrash*, as we know the Torah is true. With regard to the first claim, it is important to point out that many archaeologists do accept the Tanach as fact and use it as a basis for their ideas.

With regard to the second claim, I would like to mention that there are numerous *Rishonim* who took interest in "archaeological artifacts" to help them reach halachic conclusions. The Ramban relates that when he arrived in Acco (circa 1270) he was handed a coin with an inscription in ancient Hebrew. He had a Samaritan read the inscription which described the coin as an ancient shekel. The Ramban weighed the coin and based on this, concluded that Rashi's opinion regarding the weight of the shekel was correct. The Abarbanel and the *Kaftor vaFerach* relate similar stories.

The Tosafos Rid had harsh words for a Torah scholar who suggested, based on his understanding of earlier sources, that the city of Acco was situated in the east of Eretz Yisrael. He writes, "How weary to me are your words! Had you seen Eretz Yisrael the way I have, you would have no doubt that Acco is on the western coast of the country."

In the Gemara we have an *Amora* who identified ancient sites and drew halachic conclusions based on their measurements or environs.

The purpose of this book is not to authenticate the Megillah and/or the *midrashim* of Chazal. Nor is this book meant to resolve any halachic issues. It is meant as a tool for understanding and visualizing the events of the Megillah. For example, as I quote in the book, the *Amora* Rav Matna visited the site of the Shushan palace and described the massive pillars that he had seen there.

When I showed a prototype of this book to two *gedolei Yisrael* from New York, their response was identical. "When are you going to print this?" they asked.

Nonetheless, a word of caution is necessary. Archaeology is not an exact science. Things are constantly changing. New discoveries and advanced methods of research often cause scholars to change or modify their conclusions. It is thus possible that some of the ideas expressed in this book will not necessarily be accepted later on. Yet the main picture will not change. The palace excavated near the modern village of Shush and referred to in this book is beyond any doubt the place where the story of the Megillah occurred. While the exact identification of Achashverosh in conventional history may remain questionable, it is clear that he was one of the kings who lived in this palace.

This book is a first in more than one way. The archaeology of Megillas Esther has hardly been dealt with in any book comparing archaeological evidence with the Tanach. In the Torah world there are few, if any, books which match Jewish sources with outside sources.

We live in an era of *kiruv rechokim*. Answers are suggested for all types of questions and solutions are offered for all types of problems. Yet with regard to archaeological issues, few books deal with them comprehensively and few *kiruv* activists are familiar with them in depth. I've lectured at *kiruv* organizations which feared to deal with the archaeological issue before I arrived. They were shocked to discover how much archaeological material that matches the Tanach perfectly is available at world museums for all to see. I've led Tanach tours at world museums and the reaction is, "How come more people aren't aware of this?"

I chose to dedicate my first book to the subject of Megillas Esther, since as I mentioned before, practically no books have dealt with this topic. (Rav Avigdor Miller *zt"l* does refer to this issue in brief, but does not go into it in detail.) We must believe that Hashem preserved these ancient sites and enabled modern-day scholars to read the ancient inscriptions for our benefit.

My work on this project lasted for four years and led me to museums and libraries on three continents. The more I familiarized myself with the Persian Empire, the more amazed I became. If not for the publication deadline, this book would continue to grow.

B'ezras Hashem, this book will be the first of a series portraying Tanach and Jewish sources in light of historical, archaeological, and geographical sources.

I hope that this book will accomplish its purposes, and I pray to the Almighty, שלא יארע תקלה על ידי.

Yehuda Landy
Telzstone, Israel
Shevat 5770

Acknowledgments

As I explained in the Foreword, this book is a culmination of a four-year research project which spanned three continents. I am very indebted to all the people who assisted me each in their own way, enabling this book to finally be published.

First, I wish to thank my mother for all her input, encouragement, and help with the editing.

The complex chronological issue of the Persian Empire was sorted out with the aid of Rav Zalman Koren *shlita*, Shai Walter, Menachem Silber, Yossi Rogeznitzki, and Mitchell First.

Much of the research for this book was done at the British Museum in London. I am very indebted to the entire staff of the Middle East Department at the British Museum for all their assistance.

Special thanks to the following members of the department:

Dr. John Curtis, Keeper of the Middle East collections, for sharing his valuable time with me, answering my queries, and supplying me with photos.

Dr. Irving Finkel, Assistant Keeper, for reviewing the cuneiform material discussed in this book, and for all his other assistance.

Nigel Tallis, Curator, for helping me with material connected to the exhibition "Forgotten Empire."

Shahrokh Razmjou, for sharing with me his firsthand knowledge of the archaeological remains at Shushan and Persepolis.

The material from the French excavations at Shushan is on display at the Louvre Museum in Paris. I am very thankful to Mrs. Agnes Benoit of the Louvre, for familiarizing me with the Shushan artifacts and supplying me with relevant published material.

Thanks to the staff of the Oriental Institute at the University of Chicago, for helping me with all my queries and requests regarding their vast collection of Persepolis artifacts and material.

Thanks to Mrs. Lori Calabria from the Persepolis Fortification Archive Project, Oriental Institute, for all her assistance with the Persepolis tablets.

Special thanks to Professor Matthew Stolper of the Oriental Institute, for answering my email queries.

Special thanks to Dr. Edwin Yamauchi, Professor of history at Miami University, Ohio, for patiently answering my emails and generously sending me his articles and publications which were extremely helpful.

Special thanks to Daniel Ladiray from the French Archaeological Mission at Shushan, for generously permitting me to use some of his published material (including the cover picture) in this book.

Thanks to Jerusalem archaeologist Avner Goren for all his help over the years.

Thanks to my good friends, Zachary Prensky, Mark Scheiner, Ariel Fuss, Adrian Jacobs, Eric Sternberg, Avi Goldstein, Yitzchak Horovitz, Kollel Iyun Hadaf and Amutat Matmonei Eretz, and all others who contributed each in their own way.

For graciously supplying me with photographs, I extend my deepest appreciation and thanks to the Trustees of the British Museum, the Oriental Museum, the Persepolis Fortification Archive Project of the Oriental Institute at the University of Chicago, Dr. J. Curtis, the Brooklyn Museum of Art, Yale University Library, D. Ladiray, Google Earth, A. Benoit, Prof. E. Yamauchi, T. Hayardeni, S. White, H. Lee, R. Verhoeven, Sebastia Giralt, Y. Horovitz, and D. Collon.

Special thanks to David Yaphe of Jerusalem

who is responsible for the gorgeous graphic design, accurate typesetting, and beautiful layout of this book.

On the publishing end, I wish to thank all the staff at Feldheim Publishers who were involved in this project, especially Mrs. Numi Stern and Mrs. Deena Nataf for their superb editing job while under pressure to meet the publication deadline.

I am very indebted to R' Yaakov Feldheim for coordinating the publication end of this project. R' Yaakov literally took this project under his wing to make sure that the book met its deadline, without compromising on the quality. May Hashem enable him to continue spreading Torah throughout Klal Yisrael for many more years, in good health.

Photo Credits

© by the author
Green stone utensils (Persepolis): p. 6 (top)
Old City wall and Shushan Gate: p. 7 (top)
Nechemia wall: p. 9
Assyrian cuneiform: p. 17
Sennacherib cylinder: p. 18
Shushan *apadna* foundation tablet: p. 27
Palace reconstruction: p. 29
Apadna column base: p. 30 (top)
Cedar tree: p. 31
Transporting trees: p. 32
Susa inscription: p. 32
Persepolis foundation tablet: p. 44
Xerxes plate from Shushan: p. 48
Apadna capital: p. 50
Persepolis treasury eyestones: p. 56 (bottom right)
Shushan wall: p. 58:
Alabaster jar and fragment (both pictures): p. 67
Jewelry (various pictures): p. 68
Susa wall: p. 72
Susa lion weight: p. 75
Susa lion frieze: p. 85
Samaritan Torah: p. 90 (right)
Samaritan Mezuzah: p. 90 (left)
Assyrian scribes: p. 91

© Trustees of the British Museum
Cyrus brick: p. 4
Cyrus cylinder: p. 5 (bottom)
Artaxerxes bowl: p. 7 (bottom)
Persepolis cast copy of Xerxes sitting on his throne: p. 15
Rawlinson inscription copy: p. 41 (copied with permission from *Forgotten Empire*)
Xhantos frieze: p. 52
Alabaster floor: p. 52
Achaemenid luxury tableware: p. 55 (top)
Babylonian chronicle: p. 64
Gold finger ring: pg 76 (top)
Darius seal: p. 76 (bottom)
Babylonian month tablet: p. 77
Lachish letter: p. 89 (left)
Parshandasa seal: p. 98 (top left)
Parshandasa seal impression: p. 98 (top right)
Xerxes murder tablet: p. 101

© Yale University Library
Puru cube: p. 74 (top)

© John Curtis
Gold and silver tablets: p. 45 (top)

© Oriental Museum
Necho vessels: p. 55 (two bottom photos)
Ashurbanipal stone vessel: p. 56 (top)
Beardless attendant: p. 67
Xerxes seal reverse Persepolis tablet: p. 76
Royal Horses: p. 86

Horses and footstool: p. 87
Persepolis seal ring and stamp seal: p. 94
The king in royal garments: p. 97

© Courtesy of Persepolis Fortification Archive Project, Oriental Institute, University of Chicago
Tablet PF 700: p. 34 (top & bottom)
Tablet PF 863: p. 63

© Google Earth
Satellite picture of Persepolis: p .35 (left)
Satellite picture of Persepolis harem and palace: p .62 (bottom)
Satellite picture of Nebuchadnezzar's reconstructed palaces in Babylon: p. 66 (top)

© J. Lendering
Susa treasury: p. 75

© A. Benoit
Reconstruction of *apadna* pillars: p. 30 (bottom)

© Visual Photos
Aerial view of Susa: pp. 22-23
Aerial view of Susa: p. 79 (top)

© D. Ladiray
Cover photo
Map of palace at Shushan: p. 26
Isometric view of the Shushan palace: p. 28
King's gate at Shushan: p. 71
King's quarters at Shushan: p. 81 (bottom)

© Courtesy of Brooklyn Museum of Art
Elephantine marriage contract: p. 92

© H. Lee
Persepolis harem and stairs to Xerxes' palace: p. 69
Persepolis delegations: pp. 98 (bottom), 99 (all), 100 (all)

© E. Yamauchi
Susa and Daniel's tomb: p. 83

© Simon White
Pictures from the tomb in Hamadan: p. 103

© The Metropolitan Museum of Art / Art Resource, NY
Gold rhyton: p. 54

© T. Hayardeni
Ancient Hebrew key: p. 89 (right)

© Rob Verhoeven
Persepolis treasury relief of Xerxes: p. 46
Peresepolis harem: p. 62 (top)
Western gate of Shushan palace: p. 66
Interior of Daniel's tomb: p. 79 (bottom)
Outer courtyard of the Shushan palace: p. 85 (bottom)
Stone irrigation channels at Pasargadae: p. 88

© Sebastia Giralt
Tomb of Cyrus: p. 13
King on throne – close-up: p. 83
Tomb of Darius: p. 102 (bottom)

© Anonymous
Xerxes golden bowl: p. 49
Persepolis pillars: p. 51
Gold rhyton: p. 53
Gate of All Nations: p. 60

© Alexander
Cyrus inscription at Pasargadae: p. 21

© Y. Horovitz
Elphantine: p. 93

© D. Collon
Remains of the royal road: p. 95 (bottom)

© E.F. Schmidt
Nebuchadnezzar eyestone: p. 56 (bottom left)

Public Domain
Susa *apadna* bases: p. 47 (bottom)
Susa inner courtyard: p. 80

Licensed photographs
Section of map, p. 8: Creative Commons Attribution-Share Alike 1.0, 2.0, 2.5
Pasargadae remains, p. 12: Creative Commons Attribution-Share Alike 3.0, by dynamosquito
Behistun inscription, p. 14: Creative Commons Attribution-Share Alike 3.0, by Hapal
Ishtar Gate, p. 20: Creative Commons Share Alike 1.0
Hamadan inscription, p. 36: Creative Commons Attribution-Share Alike 3.0 Klaus-Norbert Müller
Map Achaemenid Empire, p. 45: Creative Commons Attribution-Share Alike 3.0. Source: Anton Gutsunaev
Armies of Persia and Media, p. 47 (top): Commons Attribution-Share Alike 3.0, by Arad
Reconstructed wall of Nebuchadnezzar palace, p. 65: Creative Commons Share Alike 1.0
Persepolis treasury, p. 74: the GNU Free Documentation License, Version 1.2, by GeardM
Map with royal road, p. 95 (top): Creative Commons Attribution-Share Alike 1.0, 2.0, 2.5, by Fabienkhan
Mishloach Manos, p. 98 (center): Creative Commons Attribution-Share Alike 3.0, by dynamosquito
Naksh-i-Rustam, p. 102 (top): Creative Commons Attribution-Share Alike 3.0, by Pastaitaken

PART

I

The Persian Empire in Jewish History– An Overview

Fifty-two years after the destruction of the First Beis Hamikdash by the Babylonians, the Babylonian Empire was conquered by the kings of Persia and Media. They proceeded to then conquer most of the civilized world. In a short time, the Persian and Median kings became world emperors, controlling the largest and richest empire in the history of the ancient Near East, known as the Persian Empire or the Achaemenid Empire. The Jewish people had been in exile under control of other world empires in the past. This period, however, was very different for them. All that remains with us from the other exiles such as Egypt, Assyria, and Babylonia are bitter memories of deadly wars, captivity, slavery, and subjugation in a foreign land. On the other hand, the Persian kings treated the Jews very favorably, turning this exile into a unique chapter in our long history. Shortly after the conquest of Babylonia by the Persians, the Jews who had

been living in exile in Babylonia since the latter days of the First Beis Hamikdash felt a change for the better. Under the Persian Empire they were immediately permitted to return to their land. Eventually the Persian kings also permitted them to rebuild the Beis Hamikdash and the wall around Jerusalem. The dark period of the Babylonian Exile had ended. The next chapter, the Second Beis Hamikdash period, was one of the highlights of Jewish history. The small exception to this was the dark time before the miracle of Purim. The Jewish people faced the unprecedented threat of annihilation. By Hashem's grace, the tables were turned and this low point in Jewish history led to the annual celebration of the most joyous day in the Jewish calendar, Purim. Although the Persian Empire left a very positive mark on the Jewish people, the miracle of Purim is, beyond doubt, the single most memorable event the Jews experienced during that period.

1

The Chronology of the Persian Empire according to Chazal

Chazal (the Sages of the Talmud) review the chronology of this time period in tractate *Megillah* 11b. They teach the following: First Daryavesh (Darius), the king of Media, ruled the empire for a year. He was succeeded by Coresh (Cyrus), the king of Persia, who ruled for three years. Coresh was succeeded by Achashverosh, who ruled for fourteen years. He was succeeded by his son Daryavesh. During the second year of his reign, Daryavesh permitted the Jews to rebuild the Beis Hamikdash. This was the nineteenth year of the empire and was exactly seventy years after the destruction of the First Beis Hamikdash by Nebuchadnezzar. According to the Gemara (*Avodah Zarah* 9a), the Persian Empire lasted another thirty-four years after Daryavesh's decree and was terminated by Alexander the Great. In total, this vast empire existed for fifty-two years.[1]

A. Daryavesh (Darius the Mede)

As mentioned above, Daryavesh ruled for a very short time. He became king of the empire at the age of sixty-three and ruled for only one year. It was during this time that he threw Daniel into the lions' den (see *Daniel* 6).

B. Coresh (Cyrus), the king of Persia

The empire was a joint one to be ruled by kings of Persia and Media. After the death of Daryavesh (Darius the Mede), Coresh, the king of Persia, ruled the empire. He treated the Jews favorably, and in the first year of his reign, he permitted the Jews to return to Eretz Yisrael and rebuild the Beis Hamikdash, as stated in the Book of *Ezra*, 1:1-11:

> 1 In the first year of Coresh, king of Persia, in order that the word of Hashem by the mouth

....
1. When adding together the years that different kings ruled, one-year discrepancies are common. This is because kings' years are calculated differently from calendar years, and years of reign were not always complete years.

of Yirmeyahu might be accomplished, Hashem stirred up the spirit of Coresh, king of Persia, and he made a proclamation throughout his entire kingdom, and put it also in writing, saying:

2 "So says Coresh king of Persia: All the kingdoms of the earth has Hashem, the God of heaven, given me; and He has charged me to build Him a house in Jerusalem, which is in Judea.

3 Whoever there is among you of all His people — his God be with him — let him go up to Jerusalem, which is in Judea, and build the house of Hashem, the God of Yisrael, He is the God who is in Jerusalem.

4 And whoever is left, in any place where he sojourns, let the men of his place help him with silver, and with gold, and with goods, and with livestock, beside the freewill-offering for the house of God which is in Jerusalem."

5 Then the heads of fathers' houses of Yehudah and Binyamin, and the priests, and the Leviyim, and everyone whose spirit God had stirred to go up to build the house of Hashem which is in Jerusalem, rose up.

6 And all those who were around them strengthened their hands with vessels of silver, with gold, with goods, and with livestock, and with precious things, beside all that was willingly offered.

7 Coresh the king also brought forth the vessels of the house of the Hashem, which Nebuchadnezzar had brought forth out of Jerusalem, and had put them in the house of his gods;

8 And Coresh king of Persia brought them out by the hand of Misredas (Data-Mithra) the treasurer, and counted them out to Sheshbatzar, the prince of Yehudah.

9 And this is their number: thirty basins of gold, a thousand basins of silver, twenty-nine knives;

10 Thirty bowls of gold, four hundred and ten silver bowls of a second sort, and a thousand other vessels.

11 All the vessels of gold and of silver were five thousand and four hundred. All these did Sheshbatzar bring up, when those who had been in captivity were brought up from Babylon to Jerusalem.

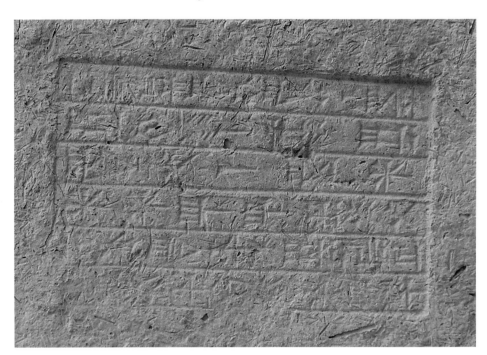

A brick from the city of Ur in southern Babylonia, with an inscription from King Coresh stating, "Cyrus king of the world... The great gods delivered all the lands into my hand." This is very similar to the language Coresh uses in the Book of *Ezra* when issuing the decree permitting the Jews to return to Eretz Yisrael. (Photograph reproduced by kind permission of the Trustees of the British Museum)

Green stone utensils from the Persepolis treasury with Aramaic inscriptions, mentioning high-ranking officials who used them. Some mention a treasurer by the name of Data-Mithra. Perhaps he is the same person mentioned here in *Ezra* 1:8.

Coresh's capital city was Babylon, from which the Babylonian kings had ruled. The country of Babylonia was situated between the Tigris and Euphrates Rivers and the inhabitants at the time included various nations who had been exiled there by the Babylonian rulers. According to *Ezra* 6:1, the decree permitting the Jews to return to their land was issued in Babylon. Excavations there uncovered a clay cylinder inscribed in cuneiform script by King Coresh. The inscription tells of Coresh's greatness and all his activities. Among them he mentioned that he permitted the nations who originated from the region east of the Tigris River to return to their original homelands and rebuild their temples that had been lying in ruins, and that he restored their idols (that had been plundered by the Babylonians).

These three decrees fit with what we know from the Book of *Ezra* regarding Coresh's actions toward the Jewish people: He permitted them to return to their homeland; he permitted them to rebuild the Beis Hamikdash; and he ordered the

The Cyrus Cylinder (photograph reproduced by kind permission of the Trustees of the British Museum)

vessels of the Beis Hamikdash to be restored.[2] The Cyrus Cylinder shows us that Coresh's permit to rebuild the Beis Hamikdash in Jerusalem was actually part of a general policy. Why did Coresh mention specifically the nations who came from east of the Tigris? What about the Jewish people who came from Eretz Yisrael, which is west of the Euphrates River? The answer is that this favorable time for the Jewish people did not last for long. In *Ezra* 4 we see that the neighbors of Judea, mainly the Samaritans, made sure to prevent the building of the Beis Hamikdash. They sent letters to the king, warning him that the rebuilding of the Beis Hamikdash would lead the Jews to revolt against the Persian king. Coresh quickly rescinded the building permit shortly after the altar had been built and the foundations of the Beis Hamikdash had been laid. This situation remained during the reign of Achashverosh. It was only during the reign of his successor, King Daryavesh, that the Jews were finally permitted to complete the Beis Hamikdash.

Midrash Shir Hashirim Rabbah (5:5) adds some more details: Shortly after Coresh permitted the Jews to return to Eretz Yisrael, he toured the financial district in Babylon and discovered that it was practically empty. When he demanded an explanation, he was told that the Jews were an integral part of the local economy. When they left Babylonia, it had a negative impact on the entire economy. [This idea is also found in archaeological evidence. Babylonian tablets from the Persian period refer to two local major banking families (Murashu and Egibi) who could conceivably be Jewish, according to Dr. Irving Finkel of the British Museum. (I thank him for bringing this to my attention.)][3] When Coresh heard this, he immediately issued a decree stating that the Jews who had already crossed the Euphrates may continue on to Judea. Those who had not yet crossed the river, however, would be turned back.

Why did he specify the Euphrates River as this travel marker? The empire was divided into twenty-three regions known as satrapies. Crossing from one satrapy to another required a permit, something similar to a passport. The Euphrates River was the border between the satrapy of Babylon and the one known as Beyond the River (עבר-נהרא; see *Ezra* 4:10, 16, 5:3, et al.). Coresh decreed that the rest of the Jews be barred from exiting the satrapy of Babylon, so as not to affect the economy any further. Perhaps this is why the Cyrus Cylinder refers only to those nations east of the Tigris River, because the permit he gave to those nations west of the Euphrates (i.e., the Jews) was later rescinded.

According to *Midrash Abba Gurion* 1:4 and *Esther Rabbah* 2:1, Coresh discovered treasures which Nebuchadnezzar had hidden in copper boats and submerged in the Euphrates River. This is also alluded to in *Yeshayahu* 45:1-3:

> **1** So said Hashem to His anointed, to Coresh whose right hand I have strengthened, to subdue nations before him…
>
> **2** "I will go before you and make the crooked places straight; I will break the doors of brass into pieces, and cut apart the bars of iron.
>
> **3** And I will give you the treasures of darkness and hidden riches of secret places…"

(See also below, p. 12)

---

2. Chazal in *Megillah* 11b state, however, that Achashverosh (who ruled after Coresh) used the vessels from the Beis Hamikdash at his party. The answer to this discrepancy is unclear. It is possible that only some of the original vessels were returned to Jerusalem, and the ones that remained in exile were later used by Achashverosh.

3. Recently, tablets with Jewish names from the post-Cyrus days have been discovered at a site named Al-Yahadu (the town of the Jews) near Borsippa in southern Iraq.

C. Achashverosh

After Coresh died, Achashverosh ruled for four-teen years. During his reign, the story of the Megillah took place, with the miracle of Purim.

D. Daryavesh

Achashverosh was succeeded by King Daryavesh, who is also referred to in *Ezra* 6:14 as Artachshaste (Artaxerxes) and Coresh (not to be confused with the Coresh mentioned earlier,

commonly known as Cyrus the Great). Daryavesh was the king who permitted the Jews to rebuild the Beis Hamikdash. It was completed during the sixth year of his reign. When the Jews built the Beis Hamikdash, they stressed the fact that it was the Persian king who had permitted them to do so, by making an image of Shushan and plac-ing it above the eastern gate of Har Habayis. The eastern gate was thus known as the Shushan Gate (*Middos* 1:3). Shortly afterwards, Ezra ascended

The current eastern wall of Har Habayis (the Temple Mount) is built on remains of the original eastern wall. The presumed location of the Shushan Gate is marked in blue on the photo. To the right, marked in red, is the sealed Old City gate, Sha'ar Harachamim. The Kidron Valley can be seen in the foreground.

Silver bowl with a royal inscription from Artaxerxes. The inscription reads: "Artaxerxes, the great king, king of kings, king of countries, son of Xerxes the king, of Xerxes [who was] the son of Darius the king, the Achaemenian, in whose house this silver drinking cup was made." (Photograph reproduced by kind permission of the Trustees of the British Museum)

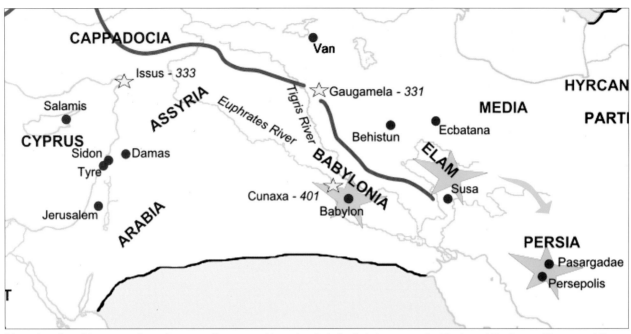

Map of ancient Mesopotamia and surrounding areas. Note that Babylonia is between the Tigris and Euphrates Rivers, and Eretz Yisrael (Israel) is to the west of the Euphrates.

to Eretz Yisrael from Babylon, and Nechemiah followed later. The two became the leaders of the Jewish people in Eretz Yisrael. Ezra focused on handling the generation's spiritual problems, while Nechemiah served as governor and rebuilt the walls of Jerusalem. He also used his powerful position to enforce Torah laws in Jerusalem and the rest of Judea.

The Gemara, in *Megillah* 12a, explains why the redemption, which began in the days of Coresh, was interrupted in the middle and only reached its completion many years later. The prophet Yirmeyahu assured the Jews that after seventy years of exile in Babylonia, they would return to Eretz Yisrael. In the Tanach we find two different references with regard to the starting point of these seventy years. In *Yirmeyahu* 29:10 the verse says, "When seventy years are completed for Babylonia I shall redeem you." The Babylonian Empire was established in the first year of Nebuchadnezzar's reign, the year he captured Nineveh (the capital city of Assyria, the previous world empire). In contrast, the Book of *Daniel* (9:2) refers to Yirmeyahu's predicting

the redemption seventy years after the destruction of Jerusalem. This event happened during the eighteenth year of Nebuchadnezzar's reign, which of course would mean that the redemption would occur only seventeen years after the first calculation. Why does Yirmeyahu seem to contradict himself? The Gemara explains that Yirmeyahu meant to say that the redemption would come in two stages. The first stage would occur seventy years after the establishment of the Babylonian Empire, and the final stage would take place seventy years after the destruction of Jerusalem. Coresh came to power seventy years after the establishment of the Babylonian Empire, but only fifty-two years after the destruction of Jerusalem. In essence, his three decrees were the first stage, enabling some of the Jews to return to Eretz Yisrael. The reconstruction of the Beis Hamikdash, however, was not meant to happen then. That is why it was delayed for many years.

The events of the Megillah occurred at a time when some Jews had already returned to Eretz Yisrael, while construction of the Beis Hamikdash

Section of the wall of Jerusalem built by Nechemiah during the days of the Persian Empire

was interrupted. The only reference to this is in the Book of *Ezra*, 4:6: "And in the reign of Achashverosh, in the beginning of his reign, they wrote an accusation against the inhabitants of Judea and Jerusalem." This appears after it mentions that the reconstruction of the Beis Hamikdash was halted from the days of Coresh until the days of Daryavesh.

According to Chazal's chronology, the second year of Daryavesh's reign came eighteen years after the Babylonian Empire was defeated by the Persians and the Medes. Darius the Mede and Coresh ruled for a total of five years.

Achashverosh ruled for fourteen years and was followed by Daryavesh. Thus Daryavesh's second year completed the seventy years since the destruction of Jerusalem, and that is the year that the construction of the Beis Hamikdash resumed.

* * *

As we have mentioned, Chazal tell us that the Jews were under the control of the Persian Empire for an additional thirty-four years after the Second Beis Hamikdash was built. It was then that Alexander the Great captured Eretz Yisrael and eventually conquered the entire Persian Empire. Thus began the era of Greek rulership.

2

Persian Kings Known to Us from Other Sources

With regard to the Persian period, conventional chronology differs greatly from Chazal's chronology. While the Gemara (*Megillah* 11b) lists only four Persian rulers, there are a total of eleven Persian kings mentioned in other sources.[4] For the purpose of our discussion, we will now delineate only the kings who can be related to those discussed by the Gemara or other Jewish sources. The difference in chronology and the identification of Achashverosh will be dealt with in Chapter 4.

A. Darius the Mede

Darius the Mede does not appear in any historical source other than the Tanach and the Gemara. It may be that no artifacts or buildings carrying his name were left behind because he only ruled for one year.

B. Cyrus the Great

Cyrus the Great, as he is known from conventional history, is beyond a doubt the Coresh we are familiar with from the Tanach. In conventional history, he is credited with defeating the Babylonians. This is not a contradiction to our sources, which place Darius the Mede ahead of Cyrus, because Jewish sources also credit Cyrus with defeating the Babylonians. Darius the Mede had joined Cyrus' forces, and an agreement was made for the Persians and the Medes to share rulership of the empire. This would be done by having a Persian king and a Median king

---

4. Greek sources list the following kings as having ruled over the Persian Empire: Cyrus (the Great), Cambyses, Darius I, Xerxes, Artaxerxes I, Xerxes II, Darius II, Artaxerxes II, Artaxerxes III, Artaxerxes IV, and Darius III. Curtis, John E. and Nigel Tallis, eds., *Forgotten Empire: The World of Ancient Persia* (London: British Museum Press, 2005), p. 264.

Remains of Cyrus' palace at Pasargadae

alternating respectively.[5] Cyrus convinced Darius that it should be the Medes who first rule the empire. This was based on Daniel's statement to Belshazzar (*Daniel* 5:28), "Your kingdom has been sliced and given to Media and Persia." Cyrus explained that since Daniel mentioned Media before Persia, the first king of the joint empire must be a Mede.

According to the Greek historian Herodotus, Cyrus diverted the waters of the Euphrates River from the city of Babylon and thus was able to conquer the city quickly, with no need for a long siege. This fits well with the *midrashim* mentioned earlier which state that Nebuchadnezzar had hid-

den away treasures in the Euphrates. We know from various inscriptions of Nebuchadnezzar that he dug many canals in the city of Babylon, filling them with water from the nearby Euphrates River. Nebuchadnezzar was well aware that these canals made the city vulnerable to the enemy. He therefore placed iron gates at the entrances to the canals to prevent an enemy from using them to access the city. According to the Midrash, he hid treasures in these canals before flooding them. When Cyrus diverted the waters of the Euphrates, he was able to enter the city via these canals, discovering the hidden treasures during the process.

....

5. Although this was the original agreement, it seems that the Persian wing eventually took over full control of the empire. It thus became known throughout history as "The Persian Empire." One of the scientific proofs for the antiquity of Megillas Esther is the fact that it always refers to Media, whose involvement was later forgotten.

Cyrus' tomb at Pasargadae as seen today

Cyrus ruled from Babylon, as we know from the accounts of the Cyrus Cylinder which was discovered there. Yet he also built himself a palace in a Persian city called Pasargadae, and after his death, he was buried there. His (empty)[6] tomb still stands in Pasargadae.

C. Cambyses

Cambyses was the son of Cyrus. The only archaeological finding connected to him is a recently discovered tomb at Pasargadae, believed to be his.

Cambyses does not appear in the Gemara. However, Rashi on *Daniel* 11:2 points out that, according to Josephus, there was an additional king by the name of Bambisha (no doubt he was referring to King Cambyses) who ruled before Achashverosh and is not mentioned by Chazal.

D. Darius the Great

After Cambyses died, the empire remained without a king for approximately a year, until Darius was eventually appointed king. He was a very powerful king who left his mark on the empire. Darius was the king who built the palace at Shushan, where the events of the Megillah occurred. (The Shushan palace will be discussed in detail in Chapter 3.) Various *midrashim*[7] do

....
6. Like most royal tombs, it was looted in ancient times, and all that remains today is the external structure.

7. E.g. *Yalkut Shimoni* 1046, *Midrash Abba Gurion* 1:2.

refer to a king by the name of Daryavesh who transferred the capital city from Babylon to Shushan. These fit well with the conventional accounts of Darius the Great.

The most important inscription Darius wrote (and probably the most important historical document surviving from the days of the entire empire) is known as the Behistun Inscription. An inscription engraved on a cliff in Behistun at the command of King Darius describes how he built the Persian Empire and how he defeated more than twenty groups of rebels during the first year of his reign. Above the text, Darius is depicted together with nine rebels who appear with nooses around their necks. A tenth rebel is lying on the ground with Darius trampling him. Behind Darius, who is the largest figure in the relief, stand two assistants who bear his weapons.

The inscription appears in cuneiform in three languages, each totaling over five hundred lines of text. (This enabled the scholars to decipher cuneiform in a manner similar to the way that the Rosetta Stone enabled scholars to decipher hiero-glyphics.) In the text, Darius writes (line 70): "Darius the king proclaims: …..this (is) the form of writing, which I have made, besides, in Aryan. Both on clay tablets and on parchment it has been placed. Besides, I also made the signature."[8] Darius' mention of parchment surely refers to papyrus. Indeed, a copy of this inscription written on papyrus has been discovered in Egypt. (The custom of writing on clay tablets versus papyrus will be discussed below, on *Esther* 8:9.)

Another major project of King Darius was the building of an additional capital city named Persepolis. (Details of the very impressive palace he built there and of the archaeological excavations will be discussed in Chapter 3.) The palace at Persepolis replaced the earlier palace at nearby Pasargadae. From then on, all the Persian kings were buried near Persepolis (see pictures below, p. 102).

E. Xerxes

The king who succeeded Darius was his son, commonly known as Xerxes. This is the way

Behistun Inscription. The text can be seen engraved on the flat walls.

....
8. Kuhrt, Amelie, *The Persian Empire* (New York: Routledge, 2007), p. 149.

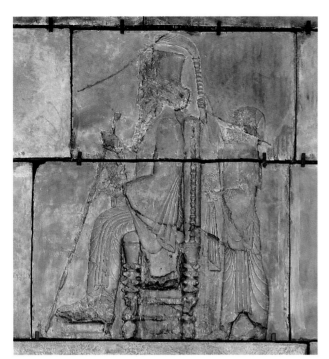

Cast copy of Persepolis relief showing King Xerxes sitting on his throne with scepter in hand (photograph reproduced by kind permission of the Trustees of the British Museum)

F. Artaxerxes

Xerxes was succeeded by his son Artaxerxes, who also continued the construction of the palaces at Shushan and Persepolis. A Persian king named Artachshaste appears in the Books of *Ezra* and *Nechemiah* and is almost certainly this same king known to us from conventional history.

* * *

The Persians did not leave us many historical documents (other than the Behistun Inscription and a few others). In the Megillah there are three references to the Persian and Median kings' book of chronicles. Unfortunately, this book has not survived.

The Persian kings continued to wage war with the Greeks for many years. Finally, in the days of Alexander the Great, the Greeks defeated the Persians and captured the empire, just as had been predicted in the Book of *Daniel*, 11:1-3:

> **1** And as for me, in the first year of Darius the Mede, I stood up to be a supporter and a stronghold to him.
>
> **2** And now I will tell you the truth. Behold, there will stand up another three kings in Persia; and the fourth shall be far richer than them all; and when he is waxed strong through his riches, he will stir up all against the kingdom of Greece.
>
> **3** And a mighty king will stand up who will rule with great dominion and do according to his will.

The Greeks, unlike the Persians, documented in detail their wars against the Persians and also referred to Persian customs and life in the king's court. Although the Greek historical records do contain some inaccuracies, they nonetheless provide considerable information, somewhat filling in the historical picture of that time. Obviously, the main interest of the Greek historians was their own history, and they did not mention other events which did not affect them. It should therefore not surprise us that they do not mention anything regarding the Jews in general or the story of Purim in particular.

the name appears in Greek historical records. In Persian, the correct pronunciation of his name is Chashiarsh, which is also how it appears in Aramaic documents from his time (חשיארש). This is one of the reasons that most scholars are convinced that Xerxes is the Achashverosh known to us from the Megillah. (This issue will be discussed at length in Chapter 4.)

Xerxes continued the construction of the palaces (both at Shushan and Persepolis), and left several inscriptions attesting to that. In the fourth year of his reign, Xerxes began a campaign against the Greeks which continued until the seventh year and failed miserably. The Persian people, however, did not view the Greeks as a threat to their empire. Instead, they viewed them as a small nation at the edge of the empire.

In Greek history, Xerxes is known mainly for this war against the Greeks. Herodotus, for example, when documenting the reign of Xerxes, focuses on the war and sums up the rest of his life in a few sentences.

3

The Archaeological Evidence

We will begin this chapter by discussing the Assyrian and Babylonian archaeological remains. Although they do not have any direct connection to the story of the Megillah, it will still be helpful to familiarize ourselves with these remains in order to understand and interpret the Persian archaeological findings.

A. Assyria

Approximately 150 years ago, the western world began discovering the archaeological sites of the ancient world. It began with the gigantic mounds in ancient Assyria (northern Iraq), which aroused the curiosity of European travelers. Eventually, excavations began on some of these mounds, which uncovered impressive remains of the Assyrian palaces from the days when the Assyrian Empire was at its peak, in the eighth and seventh centuries B.C.E. Historical accounts had been written on stone monuments, clay tablets which were stored in libraries, and clay cylinders (similar to the Cyrus Cylinder) which were deposited in foundations of palaces and temples.

Assyrian cuneiform inscription from the king's palace

The biggest obstacle for understanding these finds was the strange writing currently known as cuneiform. When cuneiform was deciphered and the inscriptions were legible, a new world was opened up. The inscriptions revealed that these mounds were the Biblical cities of Nineveh and Calah. Naturally, the most important issue for many scholars was how these finds fit with what we know from the Tanach.

When the Assyrian Empire reached its peak, it controlled all of Eretz Yisrael. At first, it captured the northern Israelite kingdom and exiled the ten tribes eastward. Later on, it also controlled the kingdom of Judea. The Assyrians left us precise, detailed records of all their wars and conquests from that time period. The records echo the Biblical accounts of these wars and often help us complete the picture. Assyrian kings known to us from the Tanach, such as Tiglat Pileser, Sargon, Sennacherib and Esarhaddon, described their victories over the Israelite kings and mentioned the taxes or tribute they received from the Israelite kings as a result. Among the names of Israelite kings that appear in Assyrian historical records are Achav, Yehu, and Menachem. Names of Judean kings mentioned include Achaz, Chizkiyahu, and Menashe. All these names are familiar to us from the Tanach.

Another very interesting source of historical information is the reliefs, or carved-out drawings, which decorated the walls of the royal palaces. They were engraved on slabs of gypsum transported to the Assyrian capitals from the hilly regions in the north of the country. These are richer than the written accounts for they include drawings of the actual battle scenes, giving us a vivid description of the events. As one would expect, these reliefs were meant to show off the might of each Assyrian king. These discoveries provided us with an unprecedented opportunity to be able to view events that are mentioned in the Tanach.

We will now focus on one set of findings which will help us determine the accuracy and credibility of the Assyrian historical records.

In Sennacherib's palace at Nineveh, a central room was dedicated to his siege and conquest of the Judean city of Lachish. It was one of

Sennacherib's major campaigns, taking place during the sixth year of his reign, in which he marched his entire army from Nineveh to Judea. He was determined to punish King Chizkiyahu for rebelling against him. In the Book of *Melachim II*, Chapters 18 and 19, the story of his campaign against Judea and Jerusalem is related. The verse does not directly mention that Sennacherib laid siege to Lachish, but it does mention that he was camped there. Shortly afterward, he set out to lay siege to Jerusalem.

Cylinder of Sennacherib (probably from Nineveh), where he mentions how he dealt with King Chizkiyahu who refused to submit to his yoke

The Nineveh reliefs depict the war against Lachish in vivid detail. They first describe the preparations of the siege, then the capture of the city, and finally the exile of its inhabitants. The artist also included the local flora and fauna together with the local scenery. The background scenery encompasses the hills of the Judean lowland as well as common fruit trees, such as the vine, fig, and olive. Anyone who visits the area of Tel Lachish (south of Beit Shemesh) today and compares the reliefs to the local scenery can easily determine where the artist sat when he documented the events. With the aid of the reliefs, excavators of Lachish were able to identify the remains of the Assyrian siege ramp.

The Assyrian kings invested massive resources to document their victories, but as one would expect, there is no mention of their setbacks. Clay cylinders from Sennacherib relate how he dealt harshly with Chizkiyahu, the king of Judea, who did not submit to his yoke. He describes how he captured forty-six walled cities and how he marched out over two hundred thousand prisoners. However, when he deals with his attack on Chizkiyahu in Jerusalem, he mentions only that he surrounded the city and threatened Chizkiyahu; he does not bother to add that 185,000 of his soldiers died suddenly, and he was forced to return quickly to Nineveh.

This is how the events are documented in *Melachim II* 19:32-37:

> **32** Therefore so says Hashem concerning the king of Assyria: 'He will not come to this city, nor shoot an arrow there; neither will he come before it with a shield, nor cast a mound against it.
>
> **33** By the way that he came he will return, and he will not come to this city, says Hashem.
>
> **34** For I will defend this city to save it, for My own sake and for My servant David's sake.'
>
> **35** And it came to pass that night, that the angel of Hashem went forth and smote in the camp of the Assyrians one hundred and eighty-five thousand; and when men arose early in the morning, behold, they were all dead corpses.
>
> **36** So Sennacherib king of Assyria departed and went and returned, and dwelled in Nineveh.
>
> **37** And it came to pass, as he was worshipping in the house of Nisroch his god, that Adrammelech and Saretzer his sons smote him with the sword; and they escaped into the land of Ararat. And Esarhaddon his son reigned in his place.

This set of remains taught us that the Assyrian historical documentation is very accurate and fairly credible, but one must also be able to read between the lines if he wants to know the complete truth. British archaeologists removed the Nineveh reliefs and transported them to London, enabling all to view them at the British Museum.

B. Babylonia

Nearly a century after Sennacherib threatened Chizkiyahu, the Assyrian Empire crumbled, and the Babylonians replaced it as the dominant world power. Nebuchadnezzar captured and sacked the Assyrian capital, Nineveh. The Babylonian capital was of course the city of Babylon. Nebuchadnezzar ruled for forty-five years, which enabled him to build palaces, city walls, temples, and water canals. Babylon was situated in a valley and thus had no stone available for construction. All the Babylonian buildings were made from baked bricks. This is evident from the story of the Tower of Babylon in *Bereishis* 11:2-3: "And it came to pass, as they journeyed east, that they found a plain in the land of Shinar; and they dwelled there. And they said one to another: 'Come, let us make bricks, and burn them thoroughly.' And they had brick for stone, and they had slime for mortar."

In the days of Nebuchadnezzar, many of the bricks manufactured were colorful and glazed. When German archaeologists excavated the city of Babylon, they found thousands of broken

fragments from the glazed bricks that were once part of the city gates and the processional way which served the Babylonians during the new year festival. The German archaeologists transported all the fragments to Berlin, where they were able to reconstruct a city gate, the processional way, and the walls from Nebuchadnezzar's throne room. One who visits the Pergamon Museum in Berlin can get an idea of Nebuchadnezzar's megalomaniac ideas from the size and grandeur of the gate and the processional way. An inscription from Nebuchadnezzar was discovered on the inner side of the gate. His name and titles were also inscribed into each brick of the palace.

In contrast to the Assyrians, the Babylonians did not leave behind many historical documents. Most of the cylinders inscribed by Nebuchadnezzar discuss his vast construction projects, but not his war campaigns. It is therefore difficult to reconstruct with accuracy the history of the Babylonian Empire. An exception to this rule is a tablet currently in the British Museum, known as the Babylonian Chronicle. This tablet was inscribed long after the events occurred and is a copy of an earlier tablet. (We will discuss the contents of this tablet below, on *Esther* 2:6.) Another Babylonian tablet lists the officers who served in Nebuchadnezzar's court. Two of those listed, Nevuzaradan and Nergal Saretzer, are known to us from *Yirmeyahu* 39:13. They participated in the conquest of Jerusalem and the destruction of the First Beis Hamikdash.

The Babylonian Empire did not exist for very long. The last king of the empire was Belshazzar. He is known to us from the story of the "writing on the wall" — "*Mena mena tekal u'farsin*" (*Daniel* 5). His reign was a short one, leaving behind only a few small cylinders which carry his name.

C. Persia

There were several capital cities during the days of the Persian and Median Empire.

As Daniel predicted to Belshazzar, the Babylonian Empire was delivered into the hands of Persia and Media. They captured the city of Babylon, and it served as their capital for some time. There are no archaeological remains of Persian palaces in Babylon. As mentioned earlier, Cyrus captured Babylon without a battle. In the Cyrus Cylinder, he describes himself not as a conqueror but rather a liberator who was welcomed by the local population. It would thus be safe to assume that the city remained intact and that the palaces of the Babylonian kings were used by the Persian kings as well.

1. Pasargadae

Cyrus built himself a second capital at a place known as Pasargadae. The remains consist of two large palaces, two small pavilions, and a gateway. A royal garden was situated in the center of the complex. (For more details on this garden and a general map of Pasargadae, see below, on *Esther* 7:7.) The plan of the palaces resembles the *apadna* at Shushan and Persepolis, described below. Trilingual inscriptions from Cyrus were also discovered there.

Trilingual inscription from Cyrus at Pasargadae

Aerial view of ancient Shushan. The impressive remains of Achashverosh's palace are clearly visible. The small castle in the foreground was built by the French archaeological mission to Shushan while excavating there over a century ago.

Although Cyrus had a palace there, Pasargadae is not referred to as a capital city in any ancient sources. Thus the function of this city remains unclear. It seems that during the reigns of Cyrus and Cambyses, Babylon was the main capital, while Pasargadae was more of a secondary royal center which later served as their burial place. Darius moved the main capital to Shushan and replaced Pasargadae with Persepolis. From then on, the kings of the empire were buried near Persepolis. What was the purpose of having two coexisting royal centers? Archaeological remains do not shed much light on this issue; we will discuss the possibilities further, in the section on Persepolis.

2. Shushan

The royal palace in the city of Shushan is the setting for the story of Megillas Esther. Clearly, by then, the capital had moved from Babylon to Shushan. It seems that the transfer occurred during the reign of Darius the Great. Presumably, he preferred ruling his vast empire from Shushan, which was more centrally located. The earliest documented identification of Shushan appears in the diary of Benjamin of Tudela (1165). He also makes mention of the tomb of Daniel which is located there. The famous Eretz Yisrael explorer Rav Ishtori HaParchi (thirteenth century) writes about Shushan as well. He did not actually travel to Persia, but rather based his knowledge of the region on information he heard from others. In his famous book *Kaftor vaFerach*, he writes (at the end of Chapter 11), "And Daniel is buried in the land of Ezra in a village named Shushtar. This is what I've been told by Rabbi … [the name does not appear] of blessed memory. It would seem to me that Shushtar is the city of Shushan." The tomb of Daniel is known nowadays in the village

of Shush in Iran, thus making it clear that this is the place mentioned by both explorers.

Approximately 150 years ago, modern-day scholars and explorers began identifying the village of Shush as the Biblical Shushan, based on the similarity of the names. Archaeological excavations began shortly afterwards and continued on and off until thirty years ago. Ancient documents found there refer to the city as Susa,[9] providing more definite confirmation that it is in fact the site of the Biblical city of Shushan.

Shushan had been the capital city of Elam (see *Daniel* 8:2) and was inhabited continuously for thousands of years. In the days of Avraham Avinu, Kedarla'omer, the king of Elam, led a campaign against the kings of Sodom and neighboring cities (*Bereishis* 14). His capital city was most likely Shushan. Archaeological excavations at Shushan have uncovered remains from all periods. The most impressive remains, however, belong to the period of the Persian Empire from the days of the kings Darius, Xerxes, and Artaxerxes. During the reign of Darius, the capital was transferred from Babylon to Shushan. It was then that Shushan was transformed from the capital of a country to the capital of a world empire.

The archaeological site, referred to as the tel (hill), at Shushan actually consists of three mounds. French archaeologists labeled them the Acropolis, the Ville Royale, and the Apadna mounds. The current shape of the tel is a result of the remodeling done in the days of Darius. When Darius moved the capital to Shushan, it underwent a major reconstruction. It was decided that all three mounds would form the royal city. First, all three sections were brought to the same height by filling in some areas (while burying earlier remains very deep) and leveling off others. The

....
9. "Susa" is the English translation of the Persian name for the city. "Shushan" is actually closer to the Persian pronunciation and will therefore be used throughout the book.

palace was built on the Apadna mound. Then, a small valley which separated the Apadna mound from the Ville Royale was deepened in order to isolate the palace from the rest of the royal city. It is unclear why very few archaeological remains were discovered on the other two mounds.

One wishing to visit the palace would have to cross over the deep ditch by means of a 30-meter (100 ft.) long bridge, finding himself in front of the very impressive "King's Gate" (see details below, on *Esther* 2:19). Beyond the gate, one would face the palace, which covered an area of 13 hectares (32 acres).

Plan of Shushan (after Curtis 2005)

The complex was basically divided into two parts: an official section and a private residence. The official section, known as the *apadna,* was where the king appeared at formal ceremonies. The private section included his personal residence and the adjacent "House of the Women".

The main building was the *apadna,* which means "palace" in Persian. The word *"apadna"* appears on an inscription discovered there. It also appears in Jewish sources such as the Book of *Daniel* (11:45) and the Gemara. Its total size was 10,000 square meters (108,000 sq. ft.). The roof of the main hall was held up by six rows of six pillars, each 20 meters (65 ft.) high. They were topped with massive capitals. A stone platform

was discovered near the southern wall of the main section. Reliefs discovered at Persepolis show the king sitting on his throne, with the heir-apparent standing behind. They both appear on a slightly elevated platform, while the rest of the people are on a lower level (see picture below, p. 46). We can assume that the platform at the Shushan palace served the same purpose, and this was the location of the throne. There were three porticoes adjacent to the *apadna* walls from the east, north, and west sides. Each portico had two rows of six columns. (The columns and their capitals will be described in detail below, on *Esther* 1:6.) The *apadna* was the site of official functions such as the new year festival (on the

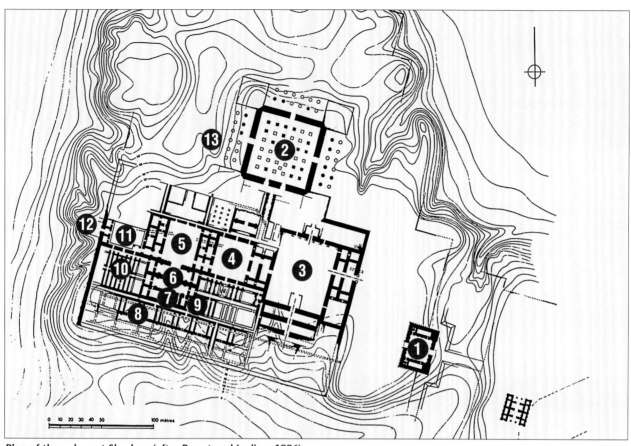

Plan of the palace at Shushan (after Perrot and Ladiray 1996)

	Section of the Palace	Reference in Megillas Esther
1	King's Gate	"At that time, when Mordechai was sitting at the king's gate" (2:21)
2	*Apadna*	Site of the large banquet (1:2-4)
3	Outer Courtyard	"Outer palace courtyard" (6:4)
4	Central Courtyard	No reference in the Megillah
5	Inner Courtyard	"The inner courtyard" (4:11, 5:1)
6	King's Apartment	"Directly facing the king's chamber" (5:1)
7	Throne Room	"The king was sitting on his royal throne... facing the entrance of the [king's] chamber" (5:1)
8	Women's House	"To the women's residence" (2:3)
9	Treasury	"And I shall have ten thousand talents of silver weighed out by the mint to be brought to the king's treasuries" (3:9)
10	Storerooms	No reference in the Megillah
11	Courtyard of the Women's House	"The courtyard of the women's residence" (2:11)
12	Western Gate	"In front of the courtyard of the women's residence" (2:11)
13	Gardens	"In the courtyard, garden [and] bisan of the king" (1:5) "The king then... [went out] to the garden of the bisan" (7:7)

first of Nisan), when representatives from all nations had to greet the king and deliver the annual tax.

The royal residence was situated south of the *apadna*. It occupied an area measuring 246 x 155 meters (807 x 510 ft.), thus covering approximately 38,000 square meters (410,000 sq. ft.). This does not include the 12,000 square meters (130,000 sq. ft.) occupied by the *apadna*. The palace was arranged around three courtyards, which decreased in size from east to west. One would enter the first gate of the royal residence via a double guardroom in order to get to the outer courtyard, which measured 64 x 55 meters (210 x 180 ft.). The doors were probably taller than 10 meters (32 ft.). From there it would be necessary to cross another double guardroom to access the central courtyard, which measured 36 x 33 meters (118 x 108 ft.). Accessing the inner courtyard would require passing through yet another double guardroom and being summoned by the king. The inner courtyard, which measured 36 x 31 meters (118 x 101 ft.), faced the king's apartment and the throne room.

Based on these archaeological findings, we can precisely pinpoint where certain events mentioned in the Megillah actually occurred.

Near the entrance to the throne room, foundation tablets were discovered. The location of their placement attests to the importance of that room. In the text of the tablets, King Darius describes in detail the effort and wealth invested when building this amazing palace. The following is a translation of the text:[10]

> This palace which I built at Susa, its ornamentation was brought from afar. The earth was dug downward, until I reached rock in the earth. When the excavation had been made, then rubble was packed down, some 40 cubits (about 58 ft.) in

The foundation tablet of the palace at Shushan

depth, another [part] 20 cubits (about 29 ft.) in depth. On that rubble the palace was constructed.

And the earth [being] dug downward, and the rubble [being] packed down, and the sun-dried brick [being] molded, the Babylonian people did [these tasks].

The cedar timber, this was brought from a mountain named Lebanon. The Assyrian people brought it to Babylon; from Babylon the Carians and the Ionians brought it to Susa. The *yakâ*-timber was brought from Gandara and from Carmania.

The gold was brought from Sardis and from Bactria, and was wrought here. The precious stone lapis lazuli and carnelian, which was wrought here, was brought from Sogdiana. The precious stone turquoise was brought from Chorasmia, [and] was wrought here.

The silver and the ebony were brought from Egypt. The ornamentation with which the wall was adorned was brought from Ionia. The ivory which was wrought here was brought from Kush (Ethiopia) and from India and from Arachosia.

The stone columns which were wrought here were brought from a village named Abirâdu, in Elam. The stone-cutters who wrought the stone, those were Ionians and Sardians.

....
10. Based on Curtis and Razmjou, "The Palace," in *Forgotten Empire*, p. 56.

The goldsmiths who wrought the gold, those were Medes and Egyptians. The men who wrought the wood, those were Sardians and Egyptians. The men who wrought the baked brick, those were Babylonians. The men who adorned the wall, those were Medes and Egyptians.

Darius the King says: At Susa a very excellent [work] was ordered, a very excellent [work] was brought to completion.

This document enables us to create the most complete reconstruction of any ancient palace. We will focus on a few points mentioned here.

The mention of "Susa" in the opening and closing statements shows us beyond any doubt that this site is indeed the site of the Biblical Shushan, based on the similarity of the names.

Darius described digging in the ground, 20 or 40 cubits deep, in order to prepare for the building of the palace. If we do the necessary calculations, we see that a terrace wall (made of bricks) was built 15 meters (49 ft.) in height. The entire area was filled with gravel. Over one million cubic meters of dirt, gravel and bricks had to be transported to the site in order to construct this massive complex.

Neither money nor effort was spared when it came to building this palace. The top materials and the best craftsmen were brought from

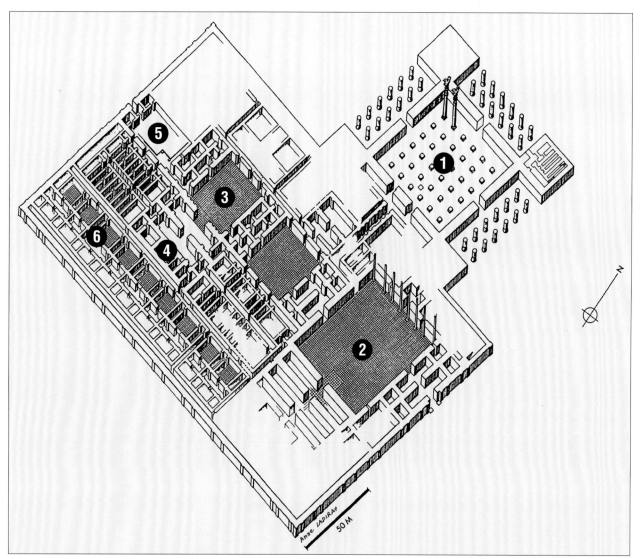

Isometric view of the Shushan palace (after Perrot and Ladiray 1996): 1. *Apadna* **2. Outer Courtyard 3. Inner Courtyard 4. Throne Room 5. Women's Courtyard 6. Women's Quarters (?)**

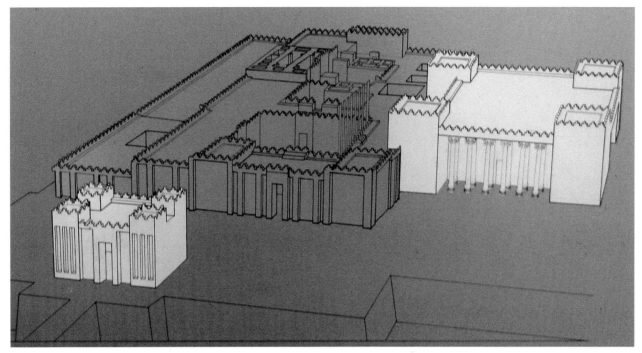
Reconstruction of the palace at Shushan

all four corners of the empire for this purpose. Darius pointed out that this palace actually represented the extent of the empire. India, Ethiopia, Sogdiana, and Sardis are the four corners of the empire, as they appear on the gold and silver foundation tablets of the Persepolis (see below, on *Esther* 1:1).

As was to be expected, the roof was made of Lebanese cedars. In the ancient world, Lebanese cedar was always the material chosen when the best roof was needed. Shlomo HaMelech built the Beis Hamikdash with Lebanese cedars. The complex operation of acquiring those cedars is described in *Melachim I* 5:15-28. (The Beis Hamikdash was also referred to as "The Lebanon.") When King Cyrus originally granted permission to rebuild the Beis Hamikdash, he also issued a special permit to transport Lebanese cedars for the roof. This is referred to in *Ezra* 3:7: "They gave money also to the hewers, and to the carpenters; and food, and drink, and oil, to the people of Tzidon, and to the people of Tzor, to bring cedar trees from Lebanon to the sea, to Yafo, according to the grant that they

had from Coresh, king of Persia."

Other kings also chose Lebanese cedars for the roofs of their temples and palaces. These include Egyptian, Assyrian, and Babylonian kings. When the prophet Yeshayahu (14:4) discusses the future downfall of Nebuchadnezzar and the Babylonian Empire, he says, "You shall take this parable against the king of Babylonia, and say: How has the oppressor ceased! The exactress of gold ceased!" He then makes reference to Nebuchadnezzar's looting of the Lebanese cedars (14:8): "Also the cypresses rejoice at you, and the cedars of Lebanon: 'Since you have lain down, no wood cutter has come up against us.'"

This was no exaggeration. A tablet inscribed by Nebuchadnezzar mentions how he captured Lebanon and "protected" it from its oppressors. No longer would Lebanon's enemies loot the lumber. Now it all belonged to Nebuchadnezzar. He said, "I organized my army for an expedition to the Lebanon. I made that country happy by eradicating its enemy everywhere." He also mentioned in detail how he overcame the physi-

Full-scale reconstruction of the base of a portico pillar of the *apadna* (Louvre Museum, Paris)

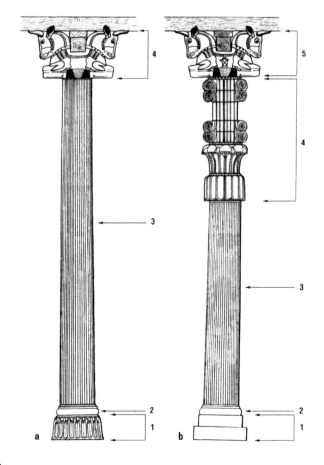

Suggested reconstruction of the *apadna* pillars. The one on the left (a) is a depiction of the pillars that were in the porticoes of the *apadna*. The base above is represented in the segment marked 1. The one on the right (b) shows what the *apadna* pillars themselves looked like. Notice the capital, segments 4 and 5. A fully reconstructed capital can be seen on p. 50.

cal obstacles when transporting the lumber from Lebanon all the way to Babylon:[11]

> What no other king had done [I achieved]: I cut through steep mountains, I split rocks, opened passages and [thus] I constructed a straight road for the [transport of these] cedars. I made the Arahtu float [down] and carry.... mighty cedars, high and strong, of precious beauty and of excellent dark quality, the abundant yield of the Lebanon, as [if they were] reed stalks [carried by] the river.

No doubt, however, the transporting of the cedars to Shushan by Darius was much more complex, as it required carrying them an additional 370 km. (230 mi.). In the Shushan foundation tablet, Darius specified who transported the cedars from Lebanon to Babylon and who transported them from Babylon to Shushan.

....
11. Perrot and Ladiray, "The Palace of Susa," in Goodnick Westenholz, Joan (ed.), *Royal Cities of the Biblical World* (Jerusalem: Bible Lands Museum, 1996), p. 254.

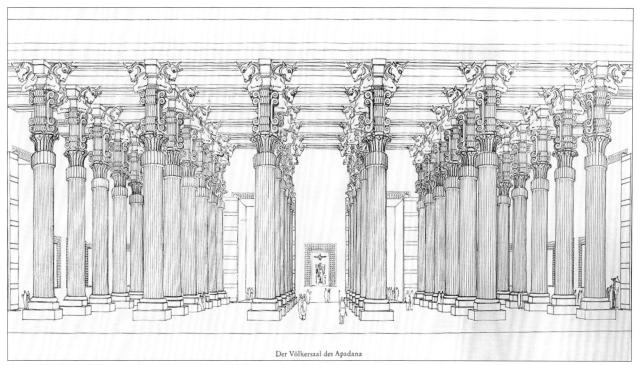

Der Völkersaal des Apadana

Reconstruction of the *apadna* at Persepolis, which was almost identical to the *apadna* at Shushan (after Krefter 1971, courtesy of Gebruder Mann Verlag)

A Lebanese cedar growing in Israel

Darius began the construction at Shushan, and it seems that his son Xerxes continued the work after he ascended the throne. Inscriptions from both kings were discovered in the remains of the palace and in other areas of the tel, some not *in situ*.

As more and more remains have been discovered, many archaeologists have also reached the conclusion that the palace at Shushan was the site for the story of the Megillah. Archaeologist Jean Perrot, who excavated the palace at Shushan and discovered the main gate to the complex, summed up an article about the palace as follows:[12]

> The Book of Esther makes Xerxes' palace at Shushan the backdrop of its story. The first excavators naturally enough tried to identify the remains they found with the setting of the Biblical account. This identification was always very vague. The gate had not been discovered, and the plan and general scheme of the palace were not understood; even the attribution of the

....
12. *Royal Cities of the Biblical World*, p. 254.

An Assyrian relief from the palace of King Sargon at Korhsabad (northern Iraq) showing how Lebanese cedars were transported on boats to be used in the building of the palace

This base was discovered in Shushan and contains an inscription from Xerxes. Evidently the construction of the palace continued during his reign.

building and its date were uncertain. Today, we have better reasons for thinking that Darius' palace at Shushan — begun in 520 B.C.E., completed by Xerxes… is indeed the palace in the mind of the author of the Book of Esther… as is evident from his descriptions of the gate, the royal apartments and perhaps the gardens.

3. Persepolis

The most impressive and most commonly known ruins from the days of the Persian Empire are those at Persepolis. Persepolis has no mention in the Megillah or in any other ancient Jewish source. It is therefore beyond the scope of this book to describe the splendor of this palace in full detail. Nonetheless, Persepolis was another capital of the Persian Empire which coexisted with and acted as a parallel to Shushan. There were thus many similarities between the structures and customs of the two palaces. For this reason, remains at Persepolis and artifacts discovered there can help shed light on our understanding of the Megillah and the palace at Shushan. Our focus will be to describe the artifacts and remains relevant to the Purim story.

Persepolis was approximately 40 km. southwest of Pasargadae and replaced it in its role as a secondary royal center (and burial place for the kings). It is actually a large complex of different buildings built by various kings of the empire. As is the case with Shushan, it was King Darius who first built there. Unlike Shushan, however, there were no earlier buildings at the site from before the days of the empire.

One of King Darius' inscriptions states, "King Darius proclaims: On this platform where this fortress has been built, previously, no fortress has been built there… And I built it, completed [it], beautified and made [it] solid, exactly as I determined."[13] The main buildings he built were his palace, an *apadna,* and the treasury. The

apadna is almost identical in its measurements to the one at Shushan. At Persepolis, some of the columns are still standing to this very day.

King Xerxes built both a larger palace and what is believed to be the women's quarters or a harem. It seems that the latter replaced an earlier building, probably built by his father Darius, which perhaps also functioned as a harem. In addition, Xerxes built the Gate of all Nations and the Hall of One Hundred Columns. Later kings also left their mark on Persepolis.

Persepolis was destroyed by Alexander the Great, as is the case with the palace in Shushan. Nonetheless, its remains are much more impressive than those at Shushan. This can be attributed to two major factors. First, the stone content at Persepolis was much higher than at Shushan. Second, Persepolis was never rebuilt after its destruction. Shushan was rebuilt numerous times, and the later construction destroyed earlier remains.

Persepolis was adorned with dozens of fascinating reliefs, many of which have survived the ages. At Shushan, none of the artwork has survived *in situ.* This is because the beautiful Persepolis reliefs were made from a local grey limestone which is very durable. The designs on the walls of the Shushan palace, on the other hand, were on colorful, glazed bricks. These designs may have been more beautiful than those at Persepolis, but they were all shattered when the palace was destroyed by Alexander the Great. (Some have been reconstructed and can be seen in Louvre Museum in Paris. See pictures below, pp. 58, 72.) Still, it is generally believed that the motifs in both palaces were similar. They show scenes from palace life, including the king sitting on his throne, royal guards, food being brought to the king's table, and the various nations bringing

....
13. *The Persian Empire*, p. 488.

the annual tax or tribute to the king. Many cuneiform inscriptions also survived at Persepolis. They are all royal inscriptions from the Persian kings known to us from the days of the empire, mainly Darius and Xerxes.

Excavations at Persepolis yielded very important finds. In the treasury, remains of weapons and armor were found, as well as valuable items made from gold, ivory, and gems. Fragments of stone utensils and other pottery were also discovered there. The most important finds in the treasury are (approximately) 750 tablets written in Elamite dating back to the end of Darius' reign, all of Xerxes' reign, and the beginning of the reign of Artaxerxes. These are known as the Persepolis Treasury tablets (PT). Near the north-east fortification walls of Persepolis, an additional 30,000 Elamite tablets were found. These are known as Persepolis Fortification tablets (PF). Only some of these have been deciphered and published. Most of them are merely administrative tablets, recording wages and rations given to workers or public servants. Nonetheless, they provide a wealth of indirect historical information. Many are inscribed on the reverse side with royal seals from the days of Darius and Xerxes, and some of the names on these tablets are Jewish names.

PF 700 is worthy of mention. The text deals

Top: PF 700, showing the name Ab-pi-ia-ma on the lower edge. According to Professor E. Yamauchi, this is equivalent to the Jewish name of Aviah. Bottom: Impression of two seals. Upper seal PFS 7, is a royal seal with a trilingual inscription from King Darius. Lower seal PFS 66c (not yet published), has an Aramaic inscription. (My thanks to Mark B. Garrison of the Oriental Institute for supplying me with this unpublished material.) Evidently, the seal was used by the recipient of the food supplies mentioned in the tablet.

with different types of flour dispensed on behalf of the king. Lines 9-10 (see picture) read "Ab-pi-ia-ma was the storekeeper." According to Prof. E. Yamauchi, Abpiiama is the Persian transliteration of the Jewish name Aviah (Abiah), which also appears in *Nechemiah* 10:8.[14] The seal (PFS 7) which appears on the reverse side (see picture) is

....
14. Yamauchi, Edwin M., *Persia and the Bible* (Grand Rapids: Baker Books, 1990, 1996), p. 372.

Satellite photo of the ruins at Persepolis (courtesy of Google Earth)

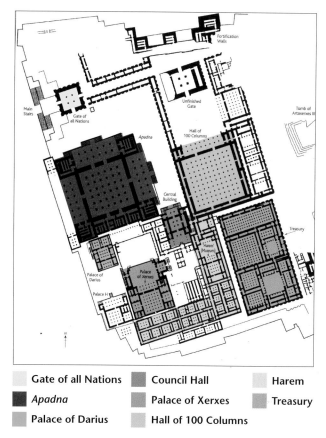

☐ Gate of all Nations	■ Council Hall		☐ Harem
■ *Apadna*	■ Palace of Xerxes		■ Treasury
■ Palace of Darius	■ Hall of 100 Columns		

Plan of the principal Persepolis buildings (after Curtis 2005)

actually a royal seal of King Darius, showing him as a hero grasping the horn of a winged bull in each hand. It also contains a trilingual inscription of the king which says, "I, Darius the king." The impression from this particular seal appears 115 times on PF tablets, all of which refer to foods dispensed "before the king" or "on behalf of the king" or other members of the royal family. It seems to have been used only by a high official in the king's court and by direct orders of the king.

A lone Elamite cuneiform ("Fortification-type") tablet was discovered in Shushan. The text is a record of oil disbursed on behalf of the king

in Shushan and five villages. Careful analyses of the impression on the tablet have shown that it was made by precisely the same seal which was used 115 times in the PF tablets.[15] The fact that this seal was used both at Shushan and Persepolis proves beyond doubt that this royal seal would travel with the king himself from place to place. It is also evident that the palace at Shushan housed a tablet archive similar to those discovered at Persepolis. Unfortunately, very few of these tablets have survived.

Another amazing discovery at Persepolis was the uncovering of four large foundation

15. Harper, Prudence O., Joan Aruz, and Francoise Talon, eds., *The Royal City of Susa* (New York: Metropolitan Museum of Art, 1992), p. 273.

Xerxes' inscription from Hamadan

tablets, two of gold and two of silver, which were inscribed by Darius. Seven foundation tablets made of stone were found nearby as well, inscribed by Xerxes. We will refer to some of these discoveries throughout the book.

Shushan and Persepolis served as capital cities simultaneously. There is no definite explanation as to exactly how the system worked. In the Tanach (*Amos* 3:15) we find the concept of kings having a winter home and a summer home. Many suggest that this was the case here. The summer climate in Shushan is unbearable. Thus, Shushan may have served as the winter palace, while Persepolis served as the summer palace. Indeed, almost all the events in the Megillah — which takes place in Shushan — happened during the winter months, between Tishrei and

Nisan. Interestingly, the number of Persepolis Fortification tablets dealing with couriers traveling to Shushan during the winter months is considerably larger than those referring to similar travel during the summer months. It is also possible that Shushan was the administrative center of the western part of the kingdom, while Persepolis dealt with the eastern half.

As is the case with the Megillah, the Greek writers of that time period made no mention of events that occurred at Persepolis. All the events they described happened at Shushan. Later writings do mention both capital cities when describing Alexander the Great's victories. Although the treasures Alexander discovered at Persepolis greatly exceeded what he found at Shushan, he still chose to celebrate his victory over the Persian Empire at Shushan, not at Persepolis. Despite the fact that he captured Persepolis after capturing Shushan, he returned to Shushan to celebrate. These points indicate that Shushan was the primary capital and was thus considered to be more distinguished than Persepolis. Persepolis was the secondary capital, like the city of Pasargadae was in the times of Cyrus and Cambyses.

Persepolis was built and occupied by the same kings who built and occupied the palace in Shushan. Some of the buildings had a similar design; the *apadna* was an actual copy. In some cases, it was the same craftsmen who worked in both places. A Persepolis Treasury tablet (PT 78) refers to a craftsman who was brought from Shushan to do work at Persepolis. It reads: "Two shekels, silver, from the treasury of Parsa (Persepolis), [which] one man, an ornament maker [and] foreman from Shushan, had come to Parsa, and for whom Barishsha was responsible. They received, etc." Since Persepolis was very similar to Shushan with regard to its architecture, occupants, and material culture (physical objects

used), we will use the archaeological remains of Persepolis (and Pasargadae) to help us portray Shushan as it was in the days of the Persian Empire.

4. Hamadan

The city of Hamadan (also known as Ecbatana; see map on p. 45) was the capital of Media. To date, no palaces from the days of the Persian Empire have been discovered there, although scholars do believe that they existed. However, other artifacts from that time period have been found in the Hamadan area. A couple of inscriptions from the days of the empire have been discovered in palaces from later periods. It would seem that Seleucid kings found these earlier remains nearby and incorporated them into their palaces. A gold foundation tablet, similar to the ones discovered at Persepolis, was found somewhere in Hamadan. There is also an inscription from Xerxes on a rock near the city.

Hamadan is also where Mordechai and Esther are buried, according to local Jewish tradition (see pictures below, p. 103).

4

Who Is Achashverosh?

We are able to identify the location of the Biblical city of Shushan and the palace, but can we identify which Persian king is the King Achashverosh mentioned in the Megillah? Seemingly this should be an easy task, for we know that Achashverosh ruled during the years 3393–3407, according to our form of counting from the year of creation. If we find the corresponding years in the Gregorian calendar, shouldn't we be able to identify him as the Persian king from those years? In reality it is not so simple, because things begin to get complicated regarding the chronology of that period. Why is this?

According to Chazal, the Second Beis Hamikdash stood for 420 years. The Gemara, in *Avodah Zarah* 9a, divides them up as follows: The first 34 years were under the Persian Empire; the next 180 years were during the Hellenistic period; 103 years were under the rule of the Maccabees; and 103 years were under the rule of the Herodian dynasty. If we add the eighteen years from the beginning of the Persian Empire until the rebuilding of the Beis Hamikdash to the thirty-four years of Persian rule after that, we get a total of fifty-two years. The number of kings listed by the Gemara as having ruled the Persian Empire during those years amounts to no more than four. They are Daryavesh (Darius the Mede), Coresh (Cyrus), Achashverosh, and Daryavesh (who is also called Artachshaste and Coresh). Cambyses (according to Rashi in the Book of *Daniel*, based on Josephus) and Darius the Great (according to several *midrashim*) may be added as well, reaching a total of six.

According to conventional history, however, the Persian Empire lasted for an additional 155 years, totaling 207 years. This is based on the Greek historians' reference to eleven Persian kings. Even with regard to those kings whose existence is agreed upon, the two sides differ regarding the length of their rule. These differences make it impossible to try and match the dates of our chronology with those of the conventional chronology as a means of associating Achashverosh with a known king of the Persian Empire.

Various *Rishonim* faced major difficulties when trying to compare historical records with Chazal's chronology. As mentioned earlier, Rashi (*Daniel* 11:2) pointed out that Josephus refers to an additional king by the name of Bambisha (i.e. Cambyses) who ruled before Achashverosh and is not mentioned in the Gemara. Radak (ibid.) also had much difficulty in trying to sort out the chronology of this time period.

This historical issue has occupied rabbis and historians for hundreds of years. Some accepted what is known today as the "Rabbinical chronology" and ignored any other evidence. Rabbi Shimon Schwab, on the other hand, was willing to accept the conventional chronology. There are yet others who tried to explain that the two chronologies do not necessarily contradict each other, and who suggested interesting theories to explain the difference.[16] It is beyond the scope of this book to deal with this issue in depth, but we will mention a few possible ways that we who accept Chazal's chronology can explain the extra names of kings that appear in history.[17]

One suggestion, based on *Rosh Hashanah* 3b, is that the Persian kings each had a number of names. One was a common name for all Persian kings, similar to "Pharaoh" in Egypt. They also had another name, which changed from king to king. The Greek historians, upon whom the conventional chronology is based, when tallying the years of the Persian Empire, considered each name individually, thus adding many extra kings and their years into the calculation.

Another suggestion is that some of the people labeled as kings were actually assistant kings with a title similar to that of a king. They were accidentally counted as kings, and their years were tallied when summing up the years of the Persian Empire.

The question remains: Which one of the eleven Persian kings in conventional sources was the King Achashverosh who is known to us from the Megillah?

As one can expect, there is no unanimous answer to this riddle. It seems that even Chazal had no undisputed answer. Nonetheless, the majority of scholars, including the noted Jewish historian, Rabbi Yitzchak Eizik Halevi Rabinowitz, identify the king commonly known as Xerxes as the King Achashverosh of the Megillah.[18] What is this conclusion based upon?

1) The events in the Megillah continue until the fourteenth year of the reign of Achashverosh. According to the Gemara, this was the final year of Achashverosh's reign. Among the list of eleven Persian Kings, Xerxes and two others ruled for close to twenty years each. The other kings either ruled for a lot less than fifteen years or a lot longer than twenty years. This already narrows down the options to Xerxes and two other kings.

2) Although his name was pronounced by the Greeks as Xerxes, the Persian pronunciation was Chashiarsh. The name appears as חשיארש in Aramaic documents from that period, discovered on the island of Elephantine in Upper Egypt. Chashiarsh, when pronounced in Hebrew, turns into Achashverosh.[19] In the Megillah, the king's name is once spelled Achashreish, which is even closer to Chashiarsh.

....

16. Chefetz, Chaim. "מלכות פרס ומדי בתקופת בית שני ולפניה; עיון מחודש" *Megadim* 14 (1991): 78-147.

17. For a discussion of the various opinions on this topic, see: First, Mitchell, *Jewish History in Conflict* (Northvale: Jason Aronson, 1997).

18. Rabinowitz, Rabbi Yitzchak Eizik Halevi, *Doros HaRishonim, Tekufas Hamikra* (Jerusalem: Dr. B. M. Lewin, 1939), p. 262.

19. The explanation for this is a bit lengthy; see: Danziger, Rabbi Shlomo Eliezer. "Who Was the Real Akhashverosh." *The Jewish Observer,* Feb. 1973: 12-15.

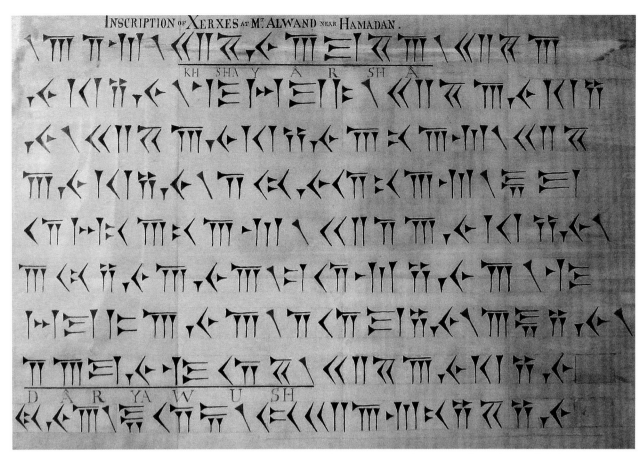

Copy of Xerxes inscription at Hamadan belonging to British scholar Sir Henry Rawlinson. Rawlinson began deciphering Persian cuneiform by studying this inscription, realizing that it must contain names of Persian kings. He identified the names of Achashverosh (pronounced Chashiarsh) and Daryavesh (pronounced Daryavush). Both names are underlined.

3) According to conventional history, the name of Xerxes' father was Darius. There are at least four places in the Midrash that refer to Achashverosh's father as Darius.[20] Archaeological evidence also shows clearly that it was Darius, the father of Xerxes, who built the palace in Shushan. According to another *midrash*,[21] it was a king by the name of Darius who moved the capital city to Shushan. This Darius must have ruled before Achashverosh since the capital was already in Shushan in Achashverosh's days. It cannot be referring to Darius the Mede because Cyrus, who ruled after him, still ruled from Babylon. There is an opinion, which also has historical basis, that he usurped Cambyses' throne and ruled during the time of Cambyses. It is very possible that building Shushan was part of his plan to take control of the empire. It is still unclear who the Darius of the Midrash is and how it can be that he does not appear in other Jewish sources. In any case, the relationship of Achashverosh to Darius is another reason that most scholars associate him with Xerxes.

....

20. E.g. *Yalkut Shimoni* 1049 and *Targum Sheini* 1:1.
21. *Yalkut Shimoni* 1046.

4) There are also events that occurred during the reign of Xerxes that fit well with the story of the Megillah. These will be mentioned later on in the book.

We chose to follow this opinion and thus preferred to present pictures of archaeological material from the Persian Empire in general and from Shushan in particular which contain the name of Xerxes. Any further mention of Achashverosh other than from Jewish sources will be referring to Xerxes.

By no means is this an absolute truth. In *Esther Rabbah* 1:3, we find the view that Achashverosh was the king known as Artaxerxes. A similar idea appears in *Pirkei d'Rabi Eliezer*.

This view also appears in early Greek translations of the Megillah and was followed by the Jewish historian Josephus.

Even so, we must keep in mind that Shushan has been indentified beyond doubt, and that the Persian Empire is surely the empire described in the Megillah. The names of kings other than Xerxes are identical with the names of other Persian kings who appear in the Tanach. Also, the material culture of this empire did not change much from one king to another. Thus presenting an artifact from this culture as proof or description of something mentioned in the Megillah is acceptable even if the artifact belonged to a king or period other than that of Achashverosh.

PART II

Excerpts from Megillas Esther with Related Historical and Archaeological Material

ESTHER 1

1 *It happened in the days of Achashverosh — he is [the same] Achashverosh who was ruling over a hundred and twenty-seven states from Hodu (India) to Kush (Ethiopia).*

As mentioned above, the majority of scholars identify Achashverosh with the Persian king known by the Greeks as Xerxes. Beyond a doubt, he was one of the most powerful Persian kings.

Who was ruling

> "Who was ruling." Rav says: He raised himself to the throne… Some say it was to his credit — there was no one fit for the throne as he; some say it was to his disgrace — that he was not fit for the throne, but by means of distributing his wealth he rose [to the throne]. (*Megillah* 11a)

This *gemara* implies that Xerxes was not the next in line to rule, but somehow made his way to the throne. This is exactly what appears in the Greek writings and is actually attested to by Xerxes himself.

According to the Greek historians, Xerxes' father Darius had older sons, and seemingly, they would precede Xerxes in line to the throne. Nonetheless, Xerxes was able to convince his father that he should be the first in line for the kingship. Darius accepted his claims and named Xerxes heir-apparent. This is also alluded to in a royal inscription discovered at Persepolis: "King Xerxes proclaims: Darius had other sons also; [but]… Darius, my father, made me the greatest after himself. When my father Darius went to his [allotted] place…I became king in my father's place."[22]

....

22. *The Persian Empire*, p. 244. (Kuhrt 2007)

A Persepolis foundation tablet inscribed by Xerxes

Regarding his qualifications as king and leader, the Greek historian Herodotus writes (specifically referring to commanding the Persian army while invading Greece): "Of all of those tens of thousands of men, for goodliness and stature there was not one worthier than Xerxes himself to hold that command."[23] We see that both ideas mentioned in the Gemara regarding Achashverosh's ascent to the throne have parallels in other historical sources discussing Xerxes.

From Hodu (India) to Kush (Ethiopia)

The Persian Empire was the largest and wealthiest empire in the history of the ancient Near East, its area covering over two million square miles. The Megillah describes its area in a short sentence, "from India (in the east) to Ethiopia (in the west)." An ancient royal inscription uses a similar expression. Excavations at Persepolis uncovered four foundation tablets — two of gold and two of silver. They were placed there by King Darius

. . . .
23. *Persia and the Bible*, p. 193. (Yamauchi 1990, 1996)

A gold and silver foundation tablet inscribed by King Darius, discovered at Persepolis

when he laid the foundations for Persepolis and were inscribed in three languages, as was common with the royal inscriptions. The following is a translated excerpt from the texts:[24]

> Darius the great king, king of kings, king of countries, son of Hystaspes, an Achaemenian.
>
> Says Darius the King: This is the kingdom which I hold, from the Scythians who are beyond Sogdiana (northeast) thence onto *Ethiopia* (southwest); and from *Sind* (southeast) thence onto Sardis (northwest).

Sind is India. The king in essence lists here the four corners of the empire. The Megillah only mentions the two southern ends, as the two northern ends are probably less important with regard to the events of the Megillah.

Herodotus describes the empire in detail, listing all the different satrapies (regions) and the amount of their annual taxes or tribute. His description of the satrapies also corresponds with, "from India to Ethiopia," although he does not actually use that phrase.

The Megillah mentions in various places that the empire totaled 127 countries. Chazal (*Esther Rabbah* 1:8) stress the connection between Queen Esther who ruled over 127 countries and our matriarch Sarah who lived for 127 years. As mentioned above, Herodotus lists only the satrapies. He does not go into detail as to how many countries were in each satrapy. The names of the more important countries do appear in Persian historical records, but we never find the names of all 127.

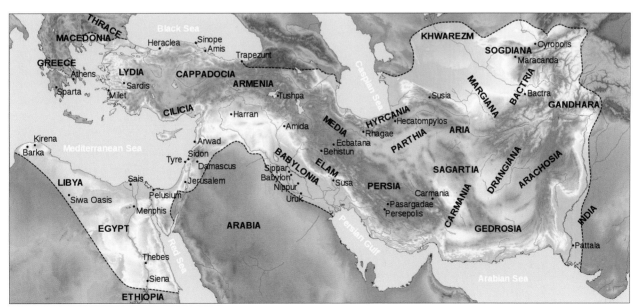

A map of the Persian Empire which extended from India to Africa

....
24. Curtis and Razmjou, "The Palace," in *Forgotten Empire*, p. 57.

A relief discovered in the treasury of the Persepolis palace. The king seated on the throne is believed to be Xerxes, and standing behind him is the heir-apparent Artaxerxes. Note that they are both on an elevated platform. This can give us a picture of the king's "seat."

2 At that time, when King Achashverosh had consolidated his rule over his kingdom, whose seat was in the citadel of Shushan. 3 In the third year of his reign, he made a banquet for all his ministers and servants, [with] the army of Persia and Media [and] the governors and ministers of the states [all] being present.

Why did Achashverosh wait until the third year of his reign to make this banquet? According to the Gemara, in *Megillah* 11b, he waited three years to be sure that the seventy years of exile promised by the prophet Yirmeyahu would expire. Until then, he was worried that when the seventy years would be completed, the Jews might rebel and rebuild the Beis Hamikdash. According to his calculation, the seventy years should have been over by the third year of his reign. When he saw that the prophecy was not fulfilled by that time, he felt secure and then began his celebration. *Midrash Abba Gurion* and the *Targum* state that the delaying of the celebration was a result of rebellions against him by various countries. World historians also tell us that Xerxes faced different rebellions during the first two years of his reign, first in Egypt and then in Babylon. Only after crushing these revolts did he have the opportunity to celebrate.

In essence, all of these ideas are similar. Achashverosh's celebration really belonged at the beginning of his reign. However, when he first ascended the throne, his grip on the empire was being challenged. Once he brought the entire empire under his strong control, he settled down and started celebrating.

The army of Persia and Media

It is written (1:3): "The army of Persia and Media," and it is written (10:2): "Of the kings of Media and Persia." [Why is Persia mentioned here first, and in the other verse Media is mentioned first?] Rava says: They stipulated with one another — If the kings are from us then the governors are from you, and if the kings are from you then the governors are from us. (*Megillah* 12a)

A Persepolis relief showing Persian and Median soldiers. They are easily distinguished by their hats: the men in the round hats are the Medes, and the Persians are wearing fluted hats. (The relief depicts two additional Median soldiers, one on each end, which do not appear in the picture.)

Remains of the *apadna* at Shushan. Mostly surviving are the bases of the massive columns which stood there during the days of the Persian Empire.

The empire was a joint partnership of the Persians and the Medes. On the Persepolis reliefs, the Persians and Medes receive equal representation. For every Persian appearing on a relief, there is a Mede appearing either on that very relief or on the relief opposite it. It is thus clear that they were equally represented in the government.

The elite unit of the Persian army was referred to as the *Ten Thousand Immortals*. They were called such because if any of them were killed or wounded, he was immediately replaced by another soldier. Thus this unit always contained ten thousand men. Although men from all of the nations controlled by the empire were required to serve in the Persian army, foreigners could not join the elite unit. The Megillah mentions that it was the soldiers from the army of Persia and Media who were called to the celebration, perhaps implying that we are referring to this elite unit, the *Immortals*. The Persian kings were known for their ability to throw a banquet for even fifteen thousand people, so it would not be out of the ordinary to invite such a large group. The *apadna* was large enough to host ten thousand people on the bottom floor alone, and it is very likely that the *apadna* was the site for the extravaganza.

4 *[This was] when he displayed the wealth of his royal glory and the magnificence of the majesty of his greatness. [The banquet lasted] for many days — 180 days.*

Achashverosh displayed his vast treasures, and it required 180 days. This was no exaggeration. Although excavations of the Shushan treasury have not yielded any valuable finds, the Greek historians relate that when Alexander the Great captured Shushan, he found forty thousand (according to others, fifty thousand) talents of silver among other valuable items (see also below, on *Esther* 1:6). At Persepolis, he discovered much more, requiring twenty thousand mules and five thousand camels to carry away all the spoils. Excavations at Persepolis show that Alexander the Great left behind some of the less important treasures, such as stone plates which were inscribed with the name of Xerxes.

Fragment of a stone plate discovered at Shushan with the name of Xerxes engraved into it

5 *And when these days ended, the king made a seven-day banquet for all the people located in the citadel of Shushan, from the greatest to the most insignificant, in the courtyard, garden [and] bisan[25] of the king.*

"In the courtyard, garden [and] *bisan* of the king." Rav and Shmuel — one says: Those who were fit for the courtyard were in the courtyard; those who were fit for the garden were in the garden; [and] those fit for the *bisan* were in the *bisan*. And [the other] one says: He [first] placed them in the courtyard, and it could not contain them; [he then placed them] in the garden, and it could not contain them, until he placed them in the *bisan* and it contained them. In a *beraisa* it was taught: He put them in the courtyard and opened two doors for them, one [entered] into the garden and one [entered] into the *bisan*. (*Megillah* 12a)

The Greek historians have a similar account. Heracleides writes:[26]

Golden bowl with the name of Xerxes engraved into it

Of those who are invited to eat with the king, some dine outdoors in full sight of anyone who wants to look on; others dine indoors with the king. Yet even these do not eat in his presence, for there are two rooms opposite each other, in one of which the king has his meal, in the other the dinner guests. But sometimes on the occasion of a public holiday, all dine in one room, in the great hall.

6 *White (chur), parsley-green and aquamarine (t'cheles) [sheets], embroidered with fine linen (butz) and purple [wool] (argaman) cords, [were spread] over silver wheels and marble pillars, [and] golden and silver couches [were set up] on a flooring of bahat, marble, dar, and sochares [stone].*

The white (*chur*), aquamarine (*t'cheles*), purple wool (*argaman*), and linen (*butz*) materials also appear in the list of royal garments with which Mordechai was adorned (see discussion there, on *Esther* 8:15). The Greek historians relate that when Alexander the Great captured Shushan, he discovered purple-dyed wool weighing five thousand talents (150 tons). Although the wool had been dyed nearly two hundred years earlier, it appeared to be as bright as if it had been freshly dyed.

Marble pillars

The Midrash, in *Esther Rabbah* 2:7, explains that these columns were of tremendous magnitude. Transporting them to the palace was a major, costly operation. According to the Midrash, the expense was so great that it would have been cheaper for the king to make the columns out of gold and silver rather than have to transport the marble columns from afar. The Midrash goes on to relate, in the name of Rav Matna, that he actually saw the marble columns. They were so big

....

25. Based on Akkadian texts, we can translate the term *"bisan"* as "a special building within a palace." (Yamauchi, Edwin M., "The Archaeological Background of Esther." *Bibliotheca Sacra*, Apr.-June 1980: 110.)

26. *The Persian Empire*, p. 160. (Kuhrt 2007)

A massive capital from the *apadna* at Shushan
(Louvre Museum, Paris)

Towering pillars at the Persepolis *apadna,* still standing after more than two millennia. The *apadna* at Shushan was built in the same style but slightly larger.

that he was able to sleep on the capital alone, while spreading out his hands and feet. The columns themselves did not survive the ages, but similar columns belonging to the *apadna* at Persepolis did. They are close to 20 meters (65 ft.) high and weigh at least twenty-five tons apiece. At Shushan, some of the capitals survived, and indeed they are large enough for a person to sleep on.

Golden and silver couches

"Golden and silver couches." Rabbi Yehudah says: Those worthy of silver were given silver, while those worthy of gold were given gold. Rabbi Nechemiah said to him: If so, you are creating jealousy at the banquet. Rather [it must mean that] the couches were made of silver and the legs were made of gold. (*Megillah* 12a)

The description of golden and silver couches, as well as other items mentioned here in connection with the king's banquet, can also be found among Greek historians. (Couches set on gold feet also appear in Greek sources; see below, on *Esther* 1:11.) The following, told by Herodotus, describes how the banquet looked in Xerxes' traveling tent. Keep in mind that this is the way he traveled, and imagine how things must have looked in the palace.[27]

Treasure there was in plenty – tents full of gold and silver furniture: couches overlaid with the same precious metals; bowls, goblets, and cups all made of gold; and wagons loaded with sacks of gold and silver basins… It is said that Xerxes on his retreat from Greece left his tent with Mardonius. When Pausanias saw it, with its

27. Simpson, "The Royal Table," in *Forgotten Empire.*

Stone relief from the Nereid monument at Xanthos (city in ancient Lydia, currently in Antalya Province, Turkey) from the days of the Persian Empire. The ruler is shown reclining on a couch with a rhyton (ancient drinking vessel) in his right hand. The form of the rhyton is typical for the Persian period (see below, on *Esther* 1:7). (Photograph reproduced by kind permission of the Trustees of the British Museum)

embroidered hangings and gorgeous decorations in silver and gold, he summoned Mardonius' bakers and cooks, and told them to prepare a meal of the same sort that they were accustomed to prepare for their former master. The order was obeyed and when Pausanias saw gold and silver couches all beautifully draped, and gold and silver tables, and everything prepared for the feast with great magnificence, he could hardly believe his eyes for the good things set before them.

A flooring of bahat

"*Bahat*" is generally identified with alabaster. In the Persian palaces, no alabaster floors have been discovered. However, earlier Assyrian palaces were found with alabaster floors. No doubt, the floors of alabaster mentioned here were similar to those discovered in Assyria.

Portion of an alabaster floor from the palace of an Assyrian king. The design is in the form of a carpet. It is very likely that there was an existing similar carpet adorning the floor. (Photograph reproduced by kind permission of the Trustees of the British Museum)

7 And [the king ordered that the guests] be given to drink in golden vessels and [other] various kinds of vessels, and [there was] much royal wine, as [befitted] the king's wealth.

Golden drinking cups, or rhytons, were common in the king's palace during the Persian period. Nowadays, there are two such rhytons surviving from that period. However, they do not contain any direct link to a king.

Alexander's general, Parmenion, sent him a list of spoils he captured from the Persians in Damascus. (This was in the days of the last Persian king, known as Darius III.) He mentioned that the total weight of golden cups taken was 73 Babylonian talents and 53 *maneh*. In metric terms, this is equivalent to 2,216.5 kg. (4,886 lbs.). When Daniel predicts that the Greeks will topple the Persian Empire, he says (*Daniel* 11:2): "And now I will tell you the truth. Behold, there will stand up another three kings in Persia; and the fourth shall be far richer than them all; and when he is waxed strong through his riches, he will stir up all against the kingdom of Greece." This gives us a glimpse of the massive wealth that the Persian Empire had accumulated.

Storing wine in golden vessels can spoil the wine; the best material for storing wine is glass. Indeed, when the Greeks mentioned the fact that the Persians drank from golden cups, they referred to it in a negative way. The Greeks preferred to drink from clay cups. However, in the Persian court, if the king sent someone wine in a clay cup, it was meant as an insult.

The Midrash also comments about drinking from golden cups:

> "And [the king ordered that the guests] be given to drink in golden vessels." All the drinks of that evil king were served in golden cups... Rabbi Pinchas said in the name of Rabbi Yitzchak: But a person despises drinking from a golden cup! It must mean that they drank from pure glass vessels...which were as costly as golden cups. (*Esther Rabbah* 2:10)

Gold rhyton from the Persian period (Tehran Museum)

In other words, the Midrash is saying that although drinking from golden cups may look nice, gold is not really the ideal material for a drinking cup. In our case, it must mean that they used glass cups, which were ideal for serving wine and were as expensive as gold in those days. Greek sources do mention the Persians' drinking from glass as well, as the Midrash describes. Remains of a glass rhyton were also discovered in the Persepolis treasury.

Various kinds of vessels
According to Chazal (*Megillah* 11b), the vessels referred to here are those which were taken to Babylon from the First Beis Hamikdash. When the Babylonian empire was captured by the Persians, these treasures made their way to the

British Museum collection of Achaemenid luxury tableware (photograph reproduced by kind permission of the Trustees of the British Museum)

Left: Gold rhyton (Metropolitan Museum of Art, New York)[28]

A vessel from the Persepolis treasury with the name of Pharaoh Necho on it

28. Vessel terminating in the forepart of a fantastic leonine creature, [lion forepart rhyton]. Iran, Hamadan possibly, 5th BCE. Achaemenid period. Gold, H. 17 cm, ¾ view. Fletcher Fund, 1954 (54.3.3). Location: The Metropolitan Museum of Art, New York, NY, U.S.A. Photo Credit: Image copyright © The Metropolitan Museum of Art / Art Resource, NY (ART323779).

treasury of the Persian kings. The Gemara in *Pesachim* (119a) adds more information:

> Rav Yehudah said in the name of Shmuel: All the gold and silver of the world was gathered by Yosef and brought to Egypt...it was there until the days of Rechav'am...Shishok the king of Egypt came and took it from Rechav'am...and it remained [in the Jewish kings' hands] until [the days of] Achaz...Sennacherib came and took it from Achaz; Chizkiyahu came and took it from Sennacherib and it remained [in the Jewish kings' hands] until Tzidkiyahu. The Babylonians came and took it from Tzidkiyahu (when the Beis Hamikdash was destroyed). [Later on] the Persians came and took it from the Babylonians.

Yalkut Shimoni (1046) and *Midrash Abba Gurion* (1:2) relate that during the reign of the Judean King Yoshiyahu, the throne of King Shlomo was captured by the Egyptian King, Pharaoh Necho, and brought to Egypt. Later, it was taken from Egypt by Nebuchadnezzar and brought to Babylon. When Coresh captured Babylon, it ended up in Persian hands. All these sources are pointing to the fact that treasures from earlier kingdoms made their way to the Persian treasury. Indeed, excavations at the Persepolis treasury yielded finds from earlier foreign kings including the Egyptian king, Pharaoh Necho; the Assyrian king, Ashurbanipal; and Nebuchadnezzar, king of Babylonia.

Stone vessel from the Persepolis treasury with the name of Assyrian king, Ashurbanipal

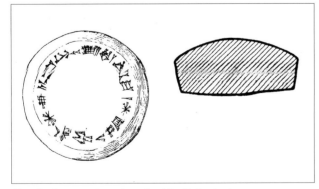

Sketch of an eyestone inscribed by Nebuchadnezzar, also discovered in the Persepolis treasury

Eyestones discovered in the Persepolis treasury. The large round black onyx eyestone in the middle was inscribed by Assyrian king Ashurbanipal.

8 *And [any amount of] drink was in order [since] there was no compulsion, for so the king had decreed upon every official of his household to carry out the [individual] wishes of each person.*

"There was no compulsion." Rabbi Elazar says: This teaches us that each man was given to drink wine that came from his own country. (*Megillah* 12a)

"There was no compulsion." – B'anpaka – [no one was compelled to drink] thick wine which was not diluted. (*Esther Rabbah* 2:13)

Both sources are pointing to the fact that the Persians would customarily force their guests to drink the local wine, which was sweet and thick and not easy to drink. In a similar vein, the Greek playwright, Aristophanes, wrote, "And those pitiless Persian hosts! They compelled us to drink sweet wine, wine without water, from gold and glass cups."[29] It is clear that the Persian customs were not acceptable to the Greeks. Here, the Megillah states that the king deviated from the custom and did not force anyone to drink something he did not want. As we see from Aristophanes, the undesired drink was the sweet and thick local Persian wine. Rabbi Elazar explains this directly by saying that, at this banquet, the king enabled everyone to drink wine that he was accustomed to from his home country.

How did Achashverosh have wine from every country in his supply? The Greek historian, Xenophon, wrote that each Persian king had vintners scouring every land to find drinks that would tickle his palate. It was also common for each country to send some of the best of its produce to the king. The Persian king made sure that the foods on his table represented the extent of the empire. For example, serving an Egyptian food at his table was meant to show that the empire included Egypt in its boundaries.

9 *Queen Vashti also made a women's banquet at King Achashverosh's royal palace.*

The Megillah mentions the names of two queens, Vashti and Esther. In all archaeological material from the Persian Empire, there is barely any mention of a queen by name. It is thus not surprising that neither Vashti nor Esther appear in any Persian records.

The Megillah stresses that Vashti hosted the women in the "royal palace." This is in contrast to the men who were hosted outside in the courtyard and/or garden. Why? The Midrash, in *Esther Rabbah* 3:10, explains that women prefer seeing beautiful artwork over eating even the fanciest foods. While the men were spending time outdoors indulging in eating and drinking, the women preferred to study the artwork on the walls of the palace.

29. Simpson, "The Royal Table," in *Forgotten Empire*.

A relief made from colorful, glazed bricks showing members of the royal guard, which adorned the walls of the Shushan palace

10 *On the seventh day, when the king was merry with wine, he told Mehuman, Bizesa, Charvona, Bigsa, Avagsa, Zesar and Karkas, the seven attendants who waited upon King Achashverosh,* **11** *to bring Queen Vashti before the king [wearing her] royal crown, to show the nations and the nobles her beauty, for she was [indeed] of fine appearance.*

According to Professor E. Yamauchi, the names Mehuman, Bigsa (Bigtha) and Karkas (Carcis) are identical to names that appear on Persepolis Fortification tablets, PF 455, 1793, and 10 respectively.[30]

It was typical of the king to summon people to drink together with him after the meal had been completed. Heracleides writes:[31]

And whenever the king orders a drinking party (which he does often), he has about a dozen companions at the symposium. When they have finished dinner — that is the king by himself, the guests in the other room — these drinking companions are summoned by one of the eunuchs. They enter and drink with him, though even they do not have the same wine; moreover, they sit on the floor, while he reclines on a couch *set on gold feet* (see above, on *Esther* 1:6).

12 *But Queen Vashti refused to come at the order of the king that [he had sent] through [his] attendants, and [so] the king was extremely enraged and his fury burned within him.*

Vashti saw the king's request as an attempt to humiliate her in public and thus refused to comply. According to *Megillah* 12a, the request for her to show up wearing the royal crown implied that she was to wear nothing else besides the crown. In general, the Persians would not display their wives in public, so this request was out of the ordinary. (In all the reliefs found in Shushan and Persepolis, no women are shown.) The Greek sources tell us that the queen would usually dine with the king in private. When the king would start drinking too much, the queen would exit, and the concubines would enter to entertain the king. Thus Achashverosh's request was a humiliating one, and Vashti had good reason to refuse. The Midrash[32] says that after Achashverosh became sober and heard what had happened, he felt that her refusal to come was justified. He was furious with his advisors for ruling the way they did.

13 *The king then consulted the wise men, experts in astronomy, for so was the king's [practice to present every] matter before all the law and judicial experts.* **14** *And his close [advisers] were Karshena, Shesar, Admasa, Tarshish, Meres, Marsena and Memuchan, the seven ministers of Persia and Media who had [constant] access to the king [and] were the highest members of the realm.*

According to Professor E. Yamauchi, the names Meres, Marsena and Memuchan (Memukan) are identical to names that appear on Persepolis

Fortification tablets, PF 760, 522, and 1344 respectively.[33]

The concept of seven advisors in the Persian

....
30. *Persia and the Bible*, p. 238.
31. *The Persian Empire*, p. 610.

32. *Esther Rabbah* 5:2, *Midrash Abba Gurion* 2:1.
33. *Persia and the Bible*, p. 238.

king's court appears numerous times in Greek historical writings; thus the Megillah's description of Achashverosh's calling upon seven close ministers to decide the fate of Vashti parallels what we know about the typical procedures in the king's court.

21 *The matter pleased the king and the ministers, and the king carried out what Memuchan had said.* 22 *He sent bills [of law] to all the king's states, to each state according to its [form of] script, and to each nation according to its language, [stating] that every man be the ruler in his house, and that [his wife] speak his language.*

He sent bills [of law] to all the king's states

It was a common practice, as can be expected, for royal decrees to be sent out to the entire empire. In the Behistun Inscription described above (see p. 14), Darius writes (line 70): "And it was written down and was read aloud before me. Afterwards, I sent off this form of writing everywhere into the countries."[34]

To each state according to its [form of] script, and to each nation according to its language

The Persian Empire was very tolerant toward other nations and respected their religion and heritage. It did not try to force its religion upon them, nor force the nations to use the Persian language and script. (This is in sharp contrast to the Greeks, who became the world power after

A royal inscription at the Gate of all Nations built by Xerxes at Persepolis. Inscribed in cuneiform, it appears in the Babylonian, Elamite, and ancient Persian languages.

....

34. *The Persian Empire*, p. 149.

the Persians. The Greeks built Greek-style cities everywhere in order to spread the Greek culture.) The Megillah stresses more than once that the king's decrees were sent out "to each country in its script and each nation in its language."

Most royal inscriptions discovered were written in three languages: Babylonian (Akkadian), Elamite and Persian. The script used for these languages was cuneiform (lit., wedge shaped). It was produced by impressing a reed stylus in moist clay to form wedge shaped markings in the clay. This writing system was developed about 2,500 years earlier. In its original form, the shapes and markings clearly depicted what the word meant. At a later period, though, the symbols became more schematic and were used to represent syllables and sounds. Elamite cuneiform derived from Babylonian and gradually took on its own appearance. The Persian script, on the other hand, was a much later development and was actually an alphabetic script (similar to the system of the Hebrew alphabet) of forty-two symbols. (Earlier syllabic cuneiform consisted of many hundreds of symbols.) Although there were fewer symbols, one had to be very knowledgeable of the Persian language in order to read the Persian cuneiform properly. Over a century ago, cuneiform was deciphered, thus enabling scholars to read all these ancient inscriptions today.

Royal inscriptions found in Egypt which originated from the Persian Empire were inscribed in hieroglyphics. Aramaic was also a prevalent language in the region of Babylonia and Eretz Yisrael and was used to relay messages to that region. (This will be discussed at length below, on *Esther* 8:9.) A stone engraved with a message from King Darius in Greek is on display at the Louvre Museum in Paris. It is thus clear that the description here in the Megillah of the king's decrees being sent out in all languages corresponds with the archaeological evidence of such a practice.

ESTHER 2

1 *After these events, when King Achashverosh's anger had abated, he remembered Vashti and what she had done, and what had been decreed upon her.* 2 *So the king's young men, his servants, said to him, "Let [the king's messengers] look for good-looking maidens for the king.* 3 *Let the king appoint officers in all the states of his kingdom, and they shall bring together every good-looking maiden to the citadel of Shushan, to the women's residence, into the charge of Hegey, the king's attendant, the guardian of the women, with their cosmetics being provided.*

The Greek historians note the vast number of concubines that the Persian kings had in their palaces. In the Shushan palace, the area assumed to be the women's and family quarters was situated in the southern section of the palace, behind the throne room, and covered an area of about 1,000 square meters (10,760 sq. ft.).[35]

....
35. Perrot and Ladiray, "The Palace of Susa," in *Royal Cities of the Biblical World*, p. 251.

One section of the women's quarters built by Xerxes at Persepolis

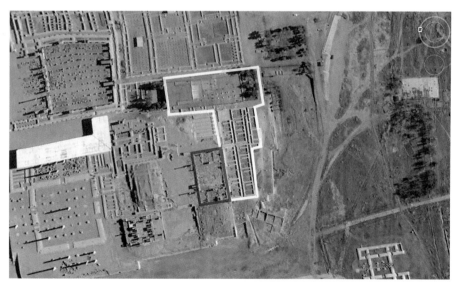

Satellite view of the southwestern area at Persepolis. The harem built by Xerxes (white framed area on right) is adjacent to his palace (blue framed area directly to the left of the harem). (Courtesy of Google Earth)

5 There was a Jewish man in the citadel of Shushan, whose name was Mordechai, the son of Ya'ir, the son of Shim'iy, the son of Kish, a man of [the tribe of] Binyamin; 6 who had been exiled from Jerusalem, with the exile that was exiled with Yechonyah, the king of Judea, whom Nebuchadnezzar, the king of Babylonia, had exiled.

Whose name was Mordechai

It is very likely that the name Mordechai was a Babylonian name. This should not surprise us, as it was common for foreigners stationed in the king's court to receive a local name. Daniel, Chananyah, Mishael, and Azaryah who served in King Nebuchadnezzar's court were also given Babylonian names (*Daniel* 1:7). Mordechai's original name was P'sachya or Bilshan (see *Menachos* 65a), but he became known by his Babylonian name, Mordechai. Perhaps this is the reason why Chazal, in *Chulin* 139b, explain that the name Mordechai has roots directly from the Torah. They were pointing out that although his name might have been Babylonian, it had Jewish significance as well.

1 cm

Tablet PF 863, one of the numerous PF tablets with the name Mordechai inscribed on it

In the Persepolis Fortification tablets, the name Mordechai appears numerous times (e.g. PF 790, 863, 941, and more). It is evident from the tablets that there were at least four different officials in the king's court bearing the name Mordechai. Are any of these tablets referring to our Mordechai, the Jew? There is no way of knowing for sure. One tablet which was discovered in the city of Borsippa and dates back to the later years of Darius or the early years of Xerxes, mentions a high official named Mordechai who was sent to inspect some matters in Shushan. According to some scholars, there is a high probability that this tablet is referring to the Mordechai who appears in the Megillah.[36]

With the exile that was exiled with Yechonyah

The story of Yechonyah's exile appears numerous times in the Tanach (e.g. *Melachim II* 24:8-17, *Divrei HaYamim II* 36:9-10). It can be summarized as follows: Eleven years before the destruction of the First Beis Hamikdash, Nebuchadnezzar came to wage war against King Yechonyah in Jerusalem because he suspected that he was not loyal to him. He offered the people a deal: If they would deliver Yechonyah into his hands, he would not wage war against the city. After the issue was discussed (probably by the Sanhedrin in the presence of the king), a decision was made to accept the deal, and King Yechonyah was delivered into the hands of Nebuchadnezzar. Nebuchadnezzar exiled

....
36. *Persia and the Bible*, p. 235.

him to Babylonia together with the spiritual and military leaders of the people. Among those exiled (then and during the previous exile a year earlier) were Mordechai, the prophet Yechezkel, Daniel, Chananyah, Mishael, and Azaryah. Nebuchadnezzar also took with him a large portion of the vessels from the Beis Hamikdash. He appointed Yechonyah's uncle to be king, named him Tzidkiyahu, and made him swear to be loyal to him. When Tzidkiyahu violated the oath and sided with Egypt, Nebuchadnezzar sent his troops to capture Jerusalem. They conquered the city, destroyed the Beis Hamikdash, and exiled almost the entire remaining population to Babylonia. Although the Babylonians did not leave us many historical documents, a tablet known as the Babylonian Chronicle tells over the activities of Nebuchadnezzar from year four to year eight of his reign. The following is the description of what Nebuchadnezzar did during the seventh year:[37]

> Year 7, Month Kislimu (Kislev): The king of Akkad (Babylonia) moved his army into Hatti land, laid siege to the city of Judah and took the city on the second day of the month Addaru (Adar). He appointed in it a [new] king of his liking, took heavy booty from it, and brought it into Babylon.

This story echoes the story of the exile of Yechonyah mentioned above. "The city of Judah" is surely referring to Jerusalem. It also appears as such one time in the Tanach (*Divrei HaYamim II* 25:18). The siege lasted no longer than three months, from the month of Kislev until the beginning of Adar. It was a short siege compared to the final siege on the city a decade later, which lasted for eighteen months. It is very likely that the reason the city was spared from a long siege and destruction was that Yechonyah surrendered peacefully. The names of the Jewish kings do not appear in the narrative. This is probably due to the fact that the tablet was copied over at a later date from an earlier tablet, and the names were not considered relevant at that later time.

Right: The reconstructed wall of the throne room at Nebuchadnezzar's palace in Babylon where Daniel, Chananyah, Mishael, and Azaryah served

The tablet known as the Babylonian Chronicle which mentions the story of the exile of King Yechonyah (photograph reproduced by kind permission of the Trustees of the British Museum)

....
37. *Ancient Near Eastern Texts*, p. 564.

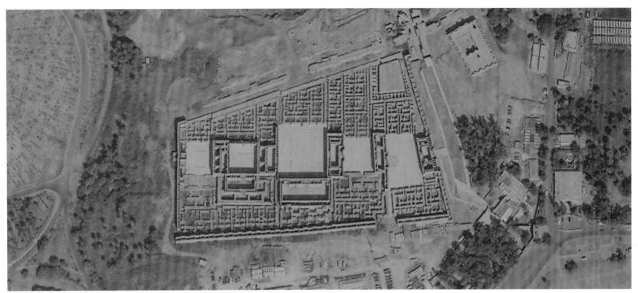
Satellite picture of Nebuchadnezzar's reconstructed palaces in Babylon (courtesy of Google Earth)

7 *He took care of Hadassah — that is Esther, his cousin — for she had no father or mother. And the girl was beautifully formed and of fine appearance, and when her father and mother died, Mordechai took her for himself as a daughter.*

Esther, like Mordechai, was a Babylonian name. In this case, however, the Megillah mentions explicitly that her original name was Hadassah. As with Mordechai, it was her Babylonian name, Esther, which remained with her. Chazal, in *Chulin* 139b, explain that the name Esther also has a Hebrew root from the Torah.

11 *And each day Mordechai would walk in front of the courtyard of the women's residence, to find out how Esther was faring and what was happening to her.*

Remains of the western gate of the palace. This was most likely the gate which led into the court of the women's quarters. It was here that Mordechai visited daily.

12 And when the time came for each girl to go to King Achashverosh — at the end of her having had the prescribed [time] for women, twelve months, for that is the duration of their cosmetic process: six months with myrrh oil and six months with perfumes and women's cosmetics.

When the British archaeologist, W.K. Loftus, excavated Shushan during the years 1850–1852, he found an unusually large amount of fragments ("enough to fill a wheelbarrow") of alabaster jars on the mound south of the palace. Some of the jars were inscribed with the name of Xerxes in various scripts.[38] It is believed that many of these jars originally contained perfume.

Alabaster jar and fragment from Shushan with Xerxes' name engraved in them. "Xerxes the great king" is written on the jar in cuneiform script (in three languages) horizontally and in hieroglyphics vertically. The fragment has the name of Xerxes in hieroglyphics.

A Persepolis relief showing an attendant with a towel in one hand and an alabaster jar in the other (perhaps containing perfume)

....

38. Curtis, "The Archaeology of the Achaemenid Period," in *Forgotten Empire*, p. 37.

13 *In this [way] the girl would go to the king: whatever she asked would be given to her, to accompany her from the women's residence to the king's palace.*

The maidens were given every opportunity to present themselves to the king in the best manner; this included being adorned with beautiful jewelry.[39] As mentioned above, no treasures from the palace itself survived *in situ*. However, in 1903, the French archaeologist, de Morgan, who excavated the Acropolis mound at Shushan, discovered a rich grave from the latter days of the Persian Empire. The coffin had originally been placed in a vaulted tomb. It contained a skeleton and a magnificent collection of jewelry, including:

a pair of gold bracelets, a pair of gold earrings, a gold torque, a pair of gold roundels, and four necklaces consisting of precious stones. Based on the size of the bones, de Morgan concluded that this was the tomb of an elderly woman. The fact that this woman was buried on the Shushan Acropolis leads us to believe that she was of royal status.

In the late 1980s, three coffins of Assyrian queens were discovered in vaulted tombs beneath the palace of Tiglat Pileser at Nimrud in Iraq;

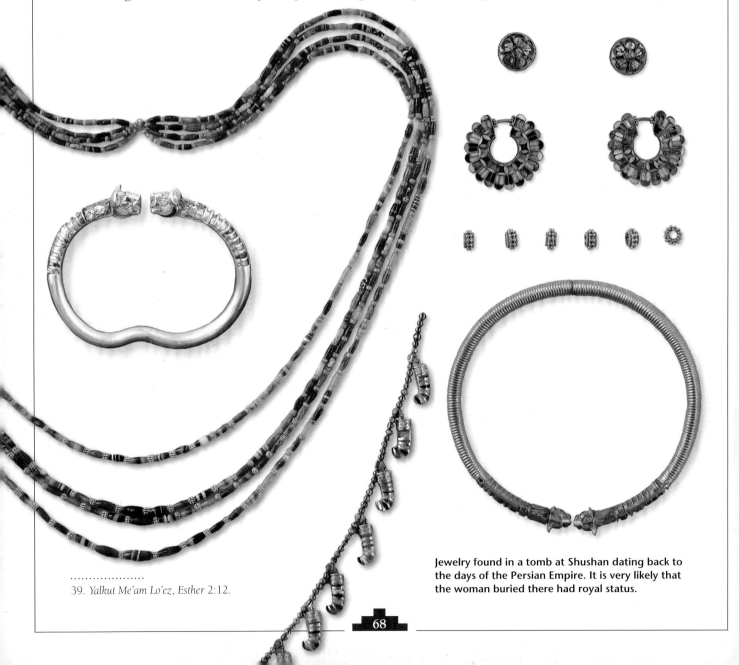

Jewelry found in a tomb at Shushan dating back to the days of the Persian Empire. It is very likely that the woman buried there had royal status.

39. *Yalkut Me'am Lo'ez, Esther 2:12.*

they were buried with their jewelry. The total weight of the gold discovered in these tombs was 38 kg. (84 lbs.). It seems that while the kings were buried in elaborate outdoor tombs for all to see, the queens were buried in the confines of the palace. It would be tempting to suggest that the tomb found at Shushan is that of Queen Esther (who, according to *Bereishis Rabbah* 39:13, was seventy-five years old when she was taken to Achashverosh). Coins found in the tomb, however, point to a period after Queen Esther's time. Nonetheless, the jewelry discovered there can give us an idea of what the jewelry was like in the Shushan palace during the days of the Megillah.

14 *In the evening she would go [to the king], and in the morning she would return to the second women's residence, into the charge of Sha'ashgaz, the king's attendant, the guardian of the concubines. She would not go again to the king, unless the king desired her and she was called by name.*

At Persepolis, the women's quarters were rebuilt by Xerxes, according to inscriptions found there. The quarters consisted of two sections arranged in the shape of an "L" which were adjacent to Xerxes' palace on the southern and eastern sides. Two stairways connected these quarters to the palace. It is very likely that one section housed the maidens while the other housed the concubines. Guard rooms were discovered near the entrance, as unauthorized entry was forbidden and punishable by death. The two sections of the women's quarters are perhaps the two sets of women's residences mentioned here in the Megillah; Hegey and Sha'ashgaz were probably situated in the guard rooms near the entrance.

Women's quarters connected by staircase to Xerxes' palace on the terrace (at Persepolis)

16 *Esther was taken to King Achashverosh, to his royal palace, in the tenth month, which is the month of Teves, in the seventh year of his reign.*

The last date mentioned in the Megillah is the third year of the king's reign, when he celebrated at the banquets. Here we are already in the seventh year. If indeed Achashverosh is Xerxes, the most plausible explanation for the lapse in time is that he was busy with his war against the Greeks during these four years (see above, p. 15).

17 *The king loved Esther more than all the [other] women, and she carried charm and favor before him more than all the [other] maidens, so he placed the royal crown on her head, and made her queen in place of Vashti.*

An image of a woman with a crown on her head can be seen on the signet ring pictured below, on *Esther* 3:10.

21 *At that time, when Mordechai was sitting at the king's [palace] gate, Bigsan and Teresh, two attendants of the king, of the guards of the inner court, were angry, and conspired to act against King Achashverosh.*

When Mordechai was sitting at the king's gate

Until this point, Mordechai would walk near the entrance of the women's courtyard, hoping to get some word about Esther's condition. Upon Esther's becoming queen, he was given an official position permitting him to sit at the king's gate. Although Mordechai's position was a minor one, Chazal consider his appointment as being an early stage of the Jews' later salvation. In the Talmud Yerushalmi, *Berachos* 1:1, the Gemara says that the future redemption of the Jewish people will happen in stages, just like the redemption brought about through Mordechai: First he sat at the king's gate, then he rode the royal horse, later he wore the royal garments, and in the end the Jews had light and happiness.

The excavations at Shushan have been going on for over a century. For many years, the archaeologists failed to locate the main gate to the palace. Only in 1970 did they finally discover its impressive remains — 80 meters (262 ft.) east of the palace itself. It was a monumental gate measuring 40 meters by 30 meters (131 x 98 ft.), a total of 1,200 square meters (13,000 sq. ft.). The gate area consisted of a main room and two side rooms (which were probably used by the guards). In the main room, bases of four columns were found. These columns, which held up the roof, presumably reached the height of 13 meters (43 ft.). On one of the bases, an inscription written in cuneiform was discovered. It reads: "King Xerxes said, King Darius my father built this palace." The gate where Mordechai sat was surely this monumental gate discovered in the Shushan excavations.

Remains of the king's gate as excavated in Shushan. The roof was held up by four columns. Two bases of the columns are shown here. One has the inscription of Xerxes.

Isometric reconstruction of the king's gate (after Perrot and Ladiray, 1996)

The guards of the inner court

Next page: A glazed brick relief of the king's personal guards from the walls of the Shushan palace. Darius mentions in his foundation tablet that it was his Babylonian subjects who produced the bricks; indeed, these bricks are very similar to those discovered at Nebuchadnezzar's palace and gate in Babylon (see pictures above, pp. 20, 65).

> **1** *After these events, King Achashverosh promoted Haman the son of Hamedasa, the Agagi, and raised his status, and made his position higher than all the [other] ministers who were with him.* **2** *And all the king's servants who were at the king's [palace] gate were bowing down and prostrating themselves to Haman, for so the king had commanded regarding him, but Mordechai would not bow down or prostrate himself.*

Archaeology has yet to yield any clues regarding the name Haman. To date, the name neither appears on any Persepolis tablets nor in any other Persian sources. The name Hamedasa, however, does appear as the name of an officer in Xerxes' court. The name is inscribed in Aramaic on green stone utensils found in the Persepolis treasury (PT5 427, PT5 492, PT5 695 and others; see picture above, p. 5). His earliest appearance is from the seventh year of the king's reign, approximately the time that Haman was promoted to his top position.

All the king's servants…were bowing down

Herodotus writes:[40]

> When the Persians encounter each other in the street, there is a way of recognizing whether those meeting are of the same rank. Because instead of hailing each other, they kiss on the mouth. If one is a little lower in status than the other, they kiss on the cheek. But if one is a great deal lower in standing than the other, he falls to the ground and pays homage to the other.

Herodotus' account can help us understand these verses. The king set the position of Haman above all the ministers and servants. The ministers who were a little lower in status than Haman were not required to bow down and prostrate, but rather to acknowledge that they were of a slightly lower status. The servants, on the other hand, were of a much lower status and were required to bow and prostrate themselves before him. This is why the Megillah stresses that the servants bowed and prostrated themselves before Haman, but does not say the same about the ministers.

> **7** *In the first month, the month of Nisan, in the twelfth year of King Achashverosh, [someone] cast pur, which is the lot, before Haman, [to select] which day and which month, [and it came out] to the twelfth month, the month of Adar.*

The lot was called a "*pur*" and later became the root for the name of the holiday "Purim." A cube inscribed in cuneiform dating back to the ninth century B.C.E. was discovered in an Assyrian palace and is known as "the lot of Yahali."[41] This cube is inscribed with the name and titles of Yahali and a prayer: "In his year assigned to him by lot (*puru*) may the harvest of the land of Assyria prosper and thrive, in front of the gods Assur and Adad may his lot (*puru*) fall." The Assyrians would apparently cast this lot, called *puru*, at the beginning of the year to determine

....

40. *The Persian Empire*, p. 624.
41. Yahali was the chief steward of King Salmanesser and was probably in charge of the ceremony of casting the lot.

the fortune of the upcoming year. We see that "pur" is an Assyrian term which was also used by the Persians, and we actually have a surviving cube to give us an authentic idea of what the Pur in the Megillah looked like.

The *puru* cube from Assyria (Yale University Museum)

> **9** *"If it pleases the king, let [a decree] be written to annihilate them, and I shall have ten thousand talents of silver weighed out by the mint to be brought to the king's treasuries."*

The weight of the Babylonian talent was 30 kg. (66 lbs.). Haman promised the king 10,000 talents of silver, which translates into 300 tons. This is an astounding figure which almost matched the annual revenue of the entire empire (based on Herodotus). It is hard to fathom that one person had accumulated such vast wealth. Indeed, Chazal, in *Esther Rabbah* 7:5, compare Haman's wealth to the legendary wealth of Korach, and label them as the two richest individuals ever.

Foreground: Ruins of the treasury at Persepolis. Background: the reconstructed section of the women's quarters.

Remains of the treasury at Shushan

A bronze weight in the form of a lion discovered at the royal complex in Shushan. Its weight is 121 kg. (267 lbs.), which was equal to four talents. At the gates of an ancient Assyrian palace, a set of sixteen similarly shaped weights was discovered. The location of the discovery suggests that they were probably the official standard. The weight found in Shushan was probably part of a set containing other, lighter weights as well.

10 *The king then removed his signet ring from his hand and gave it to Haman the son of Hamedasa, the Agagi, the oppressor of the Jews.*

A gold finger ring from the Persian period showing a woman wearing a crown. This may have been a royal signet ring. (Photograph reproduced by kind permission of the Trustees of the British Museum)

12 *The king's scribes were then summoned in the first month, on the thirteenth day of [the month], and whatever Haman commanded the king's satraps and governors who [ruled] over each state, and the ministers of each people, was written down; [to] each state according to its [form of] script, and [to] each nation according to its language. It was written in the name of King Achashverosh and sealed with the king's signet ring.*

A cuneiform tablet with a message from the king, discovered at Persepolis. The document itself is on one side, and the royal seal is impressed on the reverse side. Shown here is the impression on the back, which was made by a cylinder seal. The name Xerxes appears on the left side, and an image of the king with a crown on his head, battling two lions, appears on the right.

A royal cylinder seal (left) and modern impression (right) of King Darius discovered in Egypt. The inscription "Darius the great king" appears in three languages. Note that here too, the king is seen battling a lion. It is quite similar to King Xerxes' seal on the tablet shown above. (Photographs reproduced by kind permission of the Trustees of the British Museum)

13 *Bills [of law] were to be sent by runners to all the king's states, [ordering them] to destroy, kill and annihilate all the Jews, both young and old, children and women, on one day — the thirteenth of the twelfth month, the month of Adar — and to plunder their [property as] spoil.*

The Hebrew names of the months: Nisan, Iyar, etc., which are still in use today, appear in the Tanach only from the time of the Babylonian exile and on. During the period of the First Beis Hamikdash, the months had no names, but rather were referred to by their numerical order — first month, second month, etc. (There are some exceptions to this rule; see *Melachim I* 6:1, 38 and 8:2.) Indeed, in the Talmud Yerushalmi, *Rosh Hashanah* 1:2, Chazal tell us that "the names of the months ascended with the Jews from Babylonia." In other words, we began using these names during our exile in Babylonia and have continued using them since. Ramban on *Shemos* 12:2 explains the reason for this: Until the Exodus from Egypt, Tishrei was the first month of the year as it was the month of creation. After the Exodus, however, Nisan became the first month in order to remind us of that great miracle. When the Jews returned from Babylonia to Eretz Yisrael to build the Second Beis Hamikdash, they wanted to show their appreciation to Hashem for redeeming them. They adopted the Persian names (which originated from the Babylonians) for the months of the year, as a reminder of the redemption that occurred during the Persian period. In archaeology, we find these names in Babylonian records as far back as the El Amarna period (the days of Yaakov Avinu).

A Babylonian cuneiform tablet (front and back) listing the names of the months. They are very similar to the way we pronounce them nowadays. (Photographs reproduced by kind permission of the Trustees of the British Museum)

They are very common in inscriptions from the time of the Babylonian Empire (such as the tablet pictured above).

The names as they appear on the Babylonian tablet compared with the way we use them today:

Nisannu	Nisan
Ajaru	Iyar
Simanu	Sivan
Du'uzu	Tammuz
Abu	Av
Ululu	Elul
Tashritu	Tishrei
Arahsamnu	(Mar) Cheshvan
Kislimu	Kislev
Tebetu	Teves
Shabatu	Shevat
Addaru	Adar

15 *The runners set out in haste with the king's decree and the law was published in the citadel of Shushan. The king and Haman then sat down to drink, while [the Jews of] the city of Shushan [were] bewildered.*

The Megillah distinguishes between "the citadel (בירה) of Shushan," which is frequently mentioned, and "the city (עיר) of Shushan" (see also *Esther* 8:14-15). Remains of the palace, which was situated on the Apadna mound (see p. 25), have been found and are discussed throughout this book. This is likely what is meant by "the citadel of Shushan." The "city of Shushan," where the ordinary citizens lived, is assumed to have been located on the nearby plain, east of the mound. To date, few remains of the city from the days of the empire have been found. It is possible that more remains will be discovered in the future or that the city was composed of flimsy structures which did not survive the ages.[42]

ESTHER 4

5 *Esther then summoned Hasach, [one] of the king's attendants whom he appointed to be before her, and she instructed him about Mordechai, to find out [for] what was this [weeping], and why [he did not accept the clothes].* **6** *Hasach went out to Mordechai, to the [main] city square which was in front of the king's [palace] gate.*

According to Chazal, in *Bava Basra* 4a, Hasach was none other than Daniel. At first, Hasach is mentioned in the Megillah as the one delivering messages between Esther and Mordechai, but his name does not appear at the end of their dialogue. *Targum Sheini* (quoted in Tosafos, ibid.) explains that Haman became aware of this venue of communication and killed Hasach. Based on these two sources, we can conclude that Daniel ended his life in Shushan. The tradition identifying the tomb of Daniel in Shushan can be traced back for nearly a millennium. As mentioned above, Benjamin of Tudela and the *Kaftor vaFerach* referred to the tomb of Daniel and identified the nearby village of Shush as the Biblical Shushan.

42. Boucharlat, "Susa under Achaeminid Rule," in *Mesopotamia and Iran in the Persian Period* (London: British Museum Press, 1997), p. 66.

Top: aerial picture of modern Shusan or Shushtar. The spiral structure in the bottom lefthand corner is built over Daniel's tomb. In the background is a modern "palace," built during the French archaeological expedition to Shushan (1897–1912), which is very close to the ruins of Xerxes' palace. The palace was built in 1898; many of its bricks originated in Xerxes' palace and some have cuneiform writing on them. The picture below shows the actual shrine of Daniel's tomb.

11 *"All the king's servants and the people of the king's states know that any man or woman who comes to the king, to the inner courtyard, without being called, there is one law for him: to be put to death; only he to whom the king stretches out the golden scepter will live. I [, however,] have not been called to come to the king for the past thirty days."*

From *Esther* 5:1, we know that the inner courtyard faced the throne room (see the map there for more details of the palace layout). It is assumed that the purpose of the law prohibiting entry to the inner courtyard without being summoned was to prevent would-be assassins from getting near the king in his throne room.

The inner courtyard which faced the throne room. Note the original tiles from the time of Esther.

16 *"Go [and] gather all the Jews located in Shushan, and [proclaim a] fast on my behalf, that you will not eat and drink for three days, night and day. I, with my maids, will also fast in this way. And thus I will go to the king, [though] it is against the law, and if I perish, I perish.* **17** *Mordechai [thus] crossed over and did according to everything that Esther instructed him.*

"Mordechai [thus] crossed over." Rav says: [It means] he transgressed [God's commandment] by fasting on the first day of Passover (he fasted for three days, and the third was Passover). And Shmuel says: [It means] he crossed over a stream of water. (*Megillah* 15a)

The royal mound at Shushan is bordered on the west side by a river currently known as the Shachor River. In the days of the Tanach, the name of the river was "Ulai," as mentioned in the Book of *Daniel* (8:2): "And I saw in the vision; now it was so, that when I saw, I was in Shushan the capital, which is in the province of Elam; and I saw in the vision, and I was by the Ulai River." On the eastern side of the mound, the Persian workers dug canals and filled them with water in order to isolate the royal palace from the rest of the city. Thus, in order to notify the Jews of Shushan that they were to fast for three days, Mordechai was forced to cross this moat, or stream of water. In Pasargadae as well, there are remains of a canal that isolated the palace of Cyrus.

ESTHER 5

1 *Then, on the third day, Esther put on [her] royal [robes] and stood in the inner courtyard of the king's palace, directly facing the king's chamber, while the king was sitting on his royal throne in the royal chamber, facing the entrance of the chamber.*

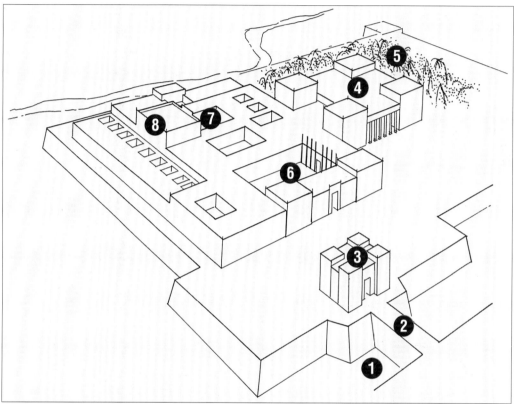

Reconstruction of the palace at Shushan: 1. Moat 2. Bridge 3. Main gate to the palace complex 4. *Apadna* 5. Gardens 6. Outer Courtyard 7. Inner Courtyard 8. Throne Room (after Perrot and Ladiray 1996)

View of the king's residence and the inner courtyard

2 *Then, when the king saw Queen Esther standing in the courtyard, she found favor in his eyes, and the king stretched out the golden scepter in his hand to Esther. Esther then approached and touched the tip of the scepter.*

Numerous Persepolis reliefs depict a king sitting on his throne. In all of them, the king is seen holding a scepter in his right hand. We thus see that the scene described here in the Megillah was typical of the Persian king's court.

King Xerxes sitting on his throne with a scepter in his right hand, as seen on this Persepolis relief

14 *Zeresh his wife, with all his friends, then said to him, "Let [the workers] make a gallows fifty cubits high, and in the morning tell the king [about it], and they shall hang Mordechai on it; and [then] go with the king to the feast feeling happy!" The idea pleased Haman and he made the gallows.*

What was the purpose of making the gallows 50 cubits high? The citadel of Shushan sat on a mound that was 15 meters tall (50 ft.; approximately thirty cubits). Haman's house was probably in the nearby city of Shushan which was situated on the plain. A 50-cubit gallows would thus rise 20 cubits over the ground level of the citadel, allowing Haman to enjoy his banquet with the king while observing his enemy hanging from the gallows.

A view from the middle court of the palace toward the southwest. Note how the upper portion of the tower above the tomb of Daniel is visible to one standing in the palace, while the rest of the modern village of Shush cannot be seen (because it is built on the plain).

ESTHER 6

1 That night, sleep eluded the king, so he asked to have the book of records, the chronicles, brought [before him], and they were read out before the king.

Why did the king's insomnia warrant reading from the king's chronicles?

> "That night, sleep eluded the king." A thought occurred to him; he said [to himself]: What could be the meaning of Esther's inviting Haman [to the party]? Perhaps they are conspiring to kill me! Then he said: Is there no friend of mine who would inform me? Then he said again: Perhaps there is a man who has done me a favor and I have not rewarded him — therefore people refrain from informing me. Immediately, he commanded [his servants] to bring before him the book of chronicles. (*Megillah* 15b)

No doubt, the request to invite Haman to the banquet was out of the ordinary. According to the Greek historians, the only people who actually dined with the king were the queen and the king's mother. The Gemara explains that this was the cause of the king's insomnia. He feared that there was a conspiracy against him, but none of his friends had bothered to notify him. The only reason he could think of for this was that he had failed to reward those who had notified him of similar plots in the past. He therefore rushed to review the chronicles to see if this was indeed the case.

Let us compare this with the words of the Greek historian, Xenophon:[43]

> We have also found that he obtained those called "the king's eyes" and "the king's ears" simply by gifts and honors. Because, by acting very generously toward those who reported matters of interest to him, he persuaded many men to listen and look carefully so they might report whatever would benefit the king. The result was that many were thought to be "the king's eyes" and "the king's ears."

But if anybody should think that the king picked one to be his "eye," he is not thinking straight — because one person would see and hear little. And it would be like telling everyone else not to pay attention if just one were appointed for this purpose. Further, if one knew that somebody was the "eye," one would know to be more careful of him.

But it is not like that, because the king listens to anybody who says that he has heard or seen something worth attention. And so there is the saying, "the king has many ears and many eyes." So everywhere people are afraid to say anything negative about the king, as though he himself were listening, or do anything bad, as though he himself were present. So not only would no one dare to say something bad about Cyrus to someone, but everyone behaved as though those who were around were all "the king's eyes" and "the king's ears." I do not know what better reason there could be for the way people behaved toward him than that he wanted to confer greater benefits in return for small ones.

The system described here was pretty simple. Anyone who reported something of interest to the king was rewarded with gifts and honor. This way there were many people willing to notify him about any possible dangers. Although Xenophon was talking about Cyrus, we can assume that this preventive system was used by the other Persian kings as well. Thus, when Achashverosh suspected that a plot was in the works and no one had warned him, he worried that this system had been disrupted. He therefore reviewed the records to make sure that he had rewarded the previous informers. When he discovered that Mordechai had not been rewarded, he immediately proceeded to reward him publicly.

---

43. *The Persian Empire*, p. 644.

4 The king then asked, "Who is in the courtyard?" and [just then] Haman had come to the outer palace courtyard, to tell the king [his wish] to hang Mordechai on the gallows that he had prepared for him. 5 The king's young men answered [the king], "It is Haman standing in the courtyard." The king said, "Let him enter!"

Upon entering the palace through two guardrooms, one would find himself in the outer courtyard (see diagram of the palace above, p. 26). This was the largest courtyard, measuring 64 x 55 meters (210 x 180 ft.). At the foot of the northern façade of the courtyard, a lion frieze was discovered by archaeologists. It has since been reconstructed and is on display in the Louvre Museum in Paris.

A lion relief which adorned the northern façade of the outer courtyard

The outer courtyard (the floor had been dug out in an attempt to reach lower levels)

8 Let [the king's servants] bring the royal robes which the king wore, and the horse on which the king rode [at his coronation], and the royal crown that was [then] placed on his head.

The verse mentions the royal crown worn by the king on his coronation day. The crown is depicted in this picture as part of a cylinder seal. The inscription reads, "I Xerxes the King." Over 100 impressions of this seal have been found at Daskyleion (northwest Anatolia). (Sketch from Kaptan 2002)

9 Let the robes and the horse then be given under the supervision of one of the king's ministers, [one] of the governors; and [the king's servants] shall dress the man whom the king wishes to honor [in the royal robes], and ride him on the horse in the [main] city square. They shall call out before him, "This is what is done to the man whom the king wishes to honor!"

The Persian royal horses were known as the "Great Nesaean" horses. According to Herodotus, the horses were called Nesaean because they were bred in a wide plain in Media of that name. The king and senior commanders rode on grey horses.[44]

Persepolis relief. Top shows the royal horses. Bottom shows alternating Persian and Median nobles.

....

44. Tallis, "Transport and Warfare," in *Forgotten Empire*, pp. 211, 217.

10 *The king then said to Haman, "Quickly take the robes and the horse, as you said, and do this to Mordechai the Jew who sits at the king's [palace] gate. Do not omit anything of whatever you said!"* **11** *Haman took the robes and the horse and dressed Mordechai [in the robes]. He then rode him in the [main] city square and called out before him, "This is what is done to the man whom the king wishes to honor!"*

The Gemara (*Megillah* 16a) tells us that when Haman told Mordechai to mount the royal horse, Mordechai replied that his fasting had made him too weak to do so on his own. Haman then bent over and allowed Mordechai to step on him in order to mount the horse. From Greek sources we know that the Persian kings were always accompanied by a servant carrying a golden footstool. The footstool enabled the king to mount and dismount his horse without having to lean on anyone or leap.[45] This is also confirmed by a Persepolis relief which shows a servant carrying a stool while standing near the royal horse. Mordechai's behavior in refusing to mount the royal horse without some form of assistance was indeed appropriate. Haman was forced to comply and humiliate himself by serving as a human footstool.

Another relief of the Persian king's royal horse. The second figure from the left is carrying the king's footstool. Note that the stool's legs have the same shape as those of the throne (see picture on p. 82). Greek historical sources relate that the footstool used was made from gold.

....
45. *The Persian Empire*, p. 540. (Kuhrt 2007)

ESTHER 7

7 The king then got up from the wine feast in a rage, [and went out] to the garden of the bisan, while Haman stood up to plead for his life from Queen Esther, for he realized that the king's bad [feelings] toward him were absolute.

The Persian gardens received honorable mention in the Greek writings. Archaeologically, it is not easy to identify ancient gardens since no ancient vegetation has survived. In Shushan there aren't many clues which can point to the location of the royal gardens. At Pasargadae, however, remains of the stone channels used to water Cyrus' gardens have been found, enabling archaeologists to reconstruct the layout of the garden. The irrigation canals divided the garden into four sections; this garden design is used in Iran even in modern times. The entire area was planted with thousands of fruit trees in straight rows (see also *Eruvin* 24a). The Persian term for the garden was the "*pardes*," a word that has made its way into Hebrew (see *Nechemiah* 2:8). The English term "paradise" also originates from the Persian *pardes*.

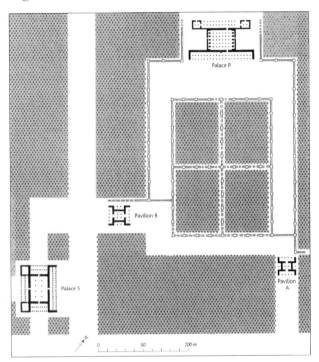

Plan of Cyrus' palaces and gardens at Pasargadae. The four boxes in the middle are divided up and surrounded by irrigation channels such as those shown in the next picture. (after Curtis 2005)

Stone irrigation channels used to water Cyrus' gardens, as discovered at Pasargadae

9 *Charvonah, one of the attendants, then said before the king, "Here is also the gallows which Haman made for Mordechai, who told over good things for the king, standing in Haman's house, 50 cubits high!" The king replied, "Hang him on it!"*

As mentioned above, the gallows, being 50 cubits tall, was visible from the king's palace. Charvonah was thus backing up his words by stating, "*Here*

is (הִנֵּה) also the gallows" and physically pointing it out to the king.

ESTHER 8

9 *At that time, in the third month, the month of Sivan, on the twenty-third of [the month], the king's scribes were summoned, and whatever Mordechai ordered concerning the Jews, and concerning the satraps, governors and ministers of the states that extended from Hodu to Kush — one hundred and twenty-seven states — was written down; [to] each state according to its [form of] script, and [to] each nation according to its language; and to the Jews, [as well,] according to their [form of] script and language.*

We discussed above the scripts and languages used in ancient Mesopotamia and Egypt. In Eretz Yisrael and its environs, an alphabetic script was used for Hebrew. This script contained twenty-two symbols which represented phonetic sounds. During the days of the First Beis Hamikdash, the

script was different from the one we use today. It is known in the Mishnah (*Yadayim* 4:5) as *ksav Ivri*, Hebrew script.[46]

The Gemara relates that during the early days of the Second Beis Hamikdash, Ezra ruled that *ksav Ashuris*, Assyrian script (which was already

An inscription written in ancient Hebrew that was discovered at the gates of Lachish and dates back to the latter days of the First Beis Hamikdash (photograph reproduced by kind permission of the Trustees of the British Museum)

Key for comparing ancient Hebrew script with modern Hebrew script

....
46. There is a debate in the Talmud Yerushalmi, *Megillah* 1:9, as to whether the *luchos* were written in *ksav Ivri* or *ksav Ashuris*. There are also different opinions (ibid. and Talmud Bavli, *Sanhedrin* 21b-22a) regarding the script used for sacred writings (e.g. *Sifrei Torah*, mezuzos) during the time of the First

Beis Hamikdash. All surviving Hebrew inscriptions from that period were written in *ksav Ivri*, yet none of them are sacred writings. Therefore, in this case, the archaeological material does not help us determine how the sacred writings were written during the First Beis Hamikdash period.

A mezuzah mounted above the entrance to a Samaritan home on Har Gerizim. It contains verses from the Torah in ancient Hebrew script, engraved into a stone.

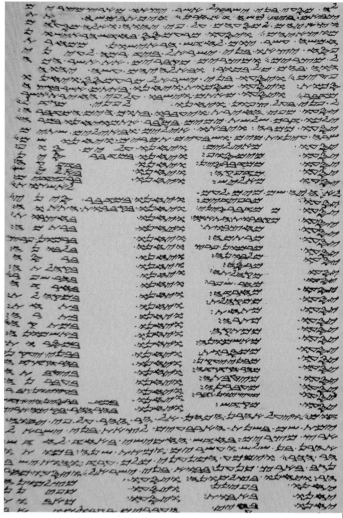

A modern-day Samaritan *Sefer Torah* written in the ancient Hebrew script

being used for other texts), should be used for the *Sefer Torah:*

> Mar Zutra, or as some say, Mar Ukva, said: Originally the Torah was given to Yisrael in Hebrew characters and in the sacred [Hebrew] language; it was given to them again in the days of Ezra in Assyrian characters and in the Aramaic language; [Finally] the Assyrian characters and the sacred [Hebrew] language were selected for Yisrael, and the Hebrew characters and the Aramaic language were left to the *Hedyotos.* Who are meant by *Hedyotos*? Rav Chisda says: The Samaritans. (*Sanhedrin* 21b)

Until this very day, the Samaritans use the ancient Hebrew script for *Sifrei Torah*, mezuzos, and prayer books, and their prayers are in Aramaic. We use the Assyrian script for writing *Sifrei Torah*, tefillin, and mezuzos, while our prayers are in Hebrew.

Our current writing format is called "Assyrian script," despite the fact that, as we mentioned earlier, all the written remains from the Assyrian Empire are in the cuneiform script and not the Assyrian script. Why is this? The Gemara (*Sanhedrin* 22a) explains: "And why is it named Assyrian? Because it was brought from the country of Assyria." In other words, when the Jewish people returned to Eretz Yisrael from Assyria during the Persian period, they took this script with them, and it thus became known as the Assyrian script. Historically speaking, the Assyrian Empire had ceased to exist at least eighty years before the

Jews returned to Eretz Yisrael. Why then is the script connected to a return "from the country of Assyria"? When Herodotus lists all the different satrapies of the Persian Empire, the satrapy of Babylonia and its vicinity was referred to as the Assyrian satrapy.[47] We see that even after the Assyrian empire ceased to exist, this area was still called Assyria. Thus when the Jews returned home to Eretz Yisrael from the "Babylonian exile," they in essence were returning from Assyria. (This is also probably the reason that "the king of Assyria" suddenly appears in the Book of *Ezra* (6:22) when discussing the return of the Jews from their exile.)

When did the Jews begin using Assyrian script? We do not have an exact answer to that question. Yet, in *Sanhedrin* 22a, Chazal tell us that this script appeared in the story of the "writing on the wall" (*Daniel* 5). That was during the reign of the Babylonian King Belshazzar, just prior to the time of Daryavesh (Darius the Mede). We can thus assume that it was already being widely used by the time of Achashverosh's reign.

The Aramaic language was also in common use in the region for many years. In the days of King Chizkiyahu, his messengers asked the Assyrian officer Ravshakeh to communicate with them in Aramaic (*Melachim II* 18:26). In the Book of *Daniel* (2:4), we see that the language used in Nebuchadnezzar's court was also Aramaic. In the Book of *Ezra* (4:7 and following chapters) we see that the language of communication between the residents of Eretz Yisrael and the Persian government was Aramaic as well.

In Assyrian art, the scribes often appear in pairs — two scribes standing side by side documenting an event. One is using a stylus and a tablet, presumably writing in cuneiform, while the other is writing on a scroll with ink, presumably in Aramaic. (They wrote Aramaic in what they called "Aramaic script," which is identical to the script we call "Assyrian.") There is reason to believe that every cuneiform tablet found in the Persepolis treasury originally had a corresponding copy written in Aramaic on papyrus. When reviewing the archaeological evidence, however, one finds very little Aramaic. Almost all the surviving written material from the ancient Near East is in cuneiform. Why is this?

As explained above, cuneiform was written by etching a stylus into wet clay. The clay

Two Assyrian scribes, one using a stylus and a clay tablet, while the second one is writing with ink on papyrus

47. Although the satrapy was originally called Babylon, it seems that things changed after Xerxes crushed a revolt there and destroyed the city of Babylon, during the early years of his reign. From then on, the satrapy became known as Assyria, for it also included the area of ancient Assyria, which was then the most important section of the satrapy.

was later hardened in the sun. If the clay tablet would be exposed to fire, it would harden even more and remain in its original form forever. Aramaic, on the other hand, was written with ink on papyrus. Papyrus is an organic material that could not survive the ages in places with a damp climate such as Babylonia, Assyria, and the Levant. It would also be destroyed by fire. Therefore it seems that when the Persepolis treasury was burned by Alexander the Great's soldiers, the cuneiform tablets hardened further and survived, but the papyrus documents were destroyed. Thus, although we know from various sources that Aramaic was used in the Assyrian, Babylonian, and Persian courts, there is very little to show for it in archaeological remains. Thirty thousand cuneiform tablets have survived the destruction of the Persepolis archives and were discovered in modern excavations; no Aramaic documents written on papyrus have been found there. Some Aramaic inscriptions, though, have been found on cylinder seals and on stone vessels used for religious purposes.

In Egypt, on the other hand, the climate is very dry. This enabled papyri from the Persian period and earlier to survive. During the days of

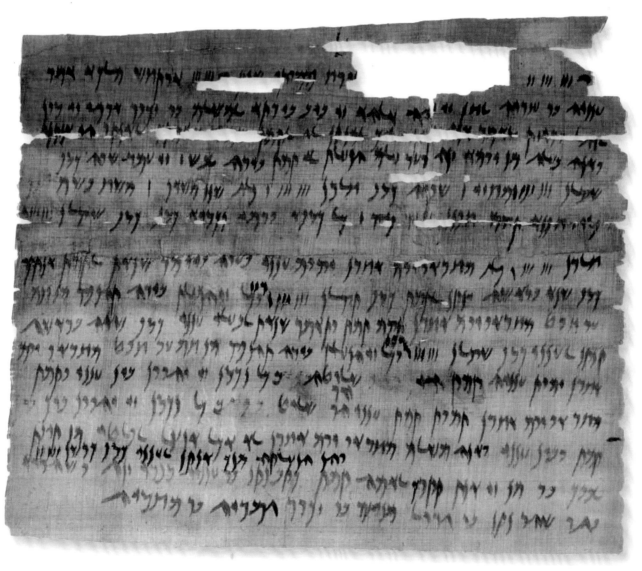

A marriage contract written in Aramaic on papyrus, from the Jewish colony at Elephantine. The date was the eighteenth of Tammuz during the sixteenth year of the reign of Artaxerexes. (After Bleiberg 2002)

Remains of the Jewish colony on the island of Elephantine in Upper Egypt. Here numerous papyri documents from the Persian period have been discovered.

the Persian Empire, a garrison of Jewish soldiers was stationed on the island of Elephantine in Upper Egypt. Excavations there uncovered papyrus documents, some of which were decrees sent in the name of the Persian king at that time. They were written in Assyrian script and in the Aramaic language. Similar documents sent to the local Egyptian population were written in the Egyptian script and language, a classic example of each nation's getting the king's decrees in its own language.

These documents also enable us to see how the Persian government treated the Jews, as they are the only surviving archaeological material from the days of the Persian Empire which have any direct reference to the Jewish people. Some were written at the command of the king and were addressed to the commander of the Jewish garrison. The tolerant policy of the Persian kings in general toward other religious groups is evident from these documents.

The following is the text of the "Passover Papyrus" found there:[48]

> To my brethren, Yedonia and his colleagues, the Jewish garrison, your brother Hananiah. The welfare of my brothers may God seek at all times. Now, this year, the fifth year of King Darius, word was sent from the king to Arsames (the Egyptian satrap) saying, "Authorize a festival of unleavened bread for the Jewish garrison." So do you count fourteen days of the month of Nisan and observe the Passover, and from the fifteenth to the twenty-first day of Nisan observe the festival of unleavened bread. Be (ritually) clean and take heed. Do no work on the fifteenth or the twenty-first day, nor drink beer, nor eat anything in which there is leaven from the fourteenth at sundown until the twenty-first of Nisan. Bring into your closets anything leavened that you may have on hand and seal it up between those dates. By order of King Darius.

> To my brethren, Yedonia and the Jewish garrison, your brother Hananiah.

The document speaks for itself. King Darius instructs the Egyptian satrap (governor) to enable the garrison of Jewish soldiers stationed at the island of Elephantine (situated at the edge of the empire) to celebrate Passover. This demonstrates what we are taught in the Tanach (*Ezra* 7:11-28) — that the Jews were given freedom of worship under the Persian rule.

Here, when the Megillah mentions that the Achashverosh's decrees were sent to the Jews in their script and in their language, we can safely assume that it is referring to Assyrian script and the Aramaic language.

....
48. *Ancient Near Eastern Texts*, p. 491.

10 *[Mordechai] had [all this] written in the name of the king, and sealed [it] with the king's signet ring. He then sent out bills [of law] with the swift horse riders [and] the riders of the king's elite express camels [and] young ponies.*

Signet ring and stamp seal discovered at Persepolis

13 *The text of the document was to become law in every state, publicized for all the nations, and for the Jews to be prepared for this day to avenge themselves of their enemies.* **14** *The swift riders, the riders of the king's elite express camels, set out in a rush and hurry with the king's decree, and the law was published in the citadel of Shushan.*

The Megillah mentions that the king's new decrees were sent out by swift riders. The Persians had developed a system that enabled them to transport the king's decrees in record time. This system included a highly developed network of roads as well as skilled riders who could ride swift horses. One famous road was called the "Royal Road" and connected the capital city of Shushan with the city of Sardis (in ancient Lydia, modern-day Turkey) — which was at the edge of the empire. Herodotus describes the course of this road in detail and mentions how much time it would take for an average person to travel each segment of the road. In total, it should have taken ninety days to travel from Shushan to Sardis. However, high-speed riders were able to cover the entire distance in record time. (Herodotus' praise for this system actually served as an inspiration to the United States Postal Service many years later.) He writes:[49]

There is nothing in the world which travels faster than these Persian couriers… It is said that men and horses are stationed along the road, equal in number to the number of days the journey takes — a man and horse for each day. Nothing stops these couriers from covering their allotted stage in the quickest time possible — neither snow, rain, heat nor darkness.

The first courier, upon completing his stage, passed the message on to the next one, who would then cover his stage and pass it on to the next courier. It is believed that, in this manner, the king's orders and decrees could reach anywhere in the empire in no more than two weeks.

While Herodotus discusses only the road with which he was familiar, i.e., the Royal Road connecting Shushan to Sardis, it is obvious that there were other high-speed roads connecting the other sections of the empire. One road connected the two capital cities of Shushan and Persepolis, other roads accessed Egypt and Ethiopia in the

....
49. Tallis, "Transport and Warfare," in *Forgotten Empire*, p. 213.

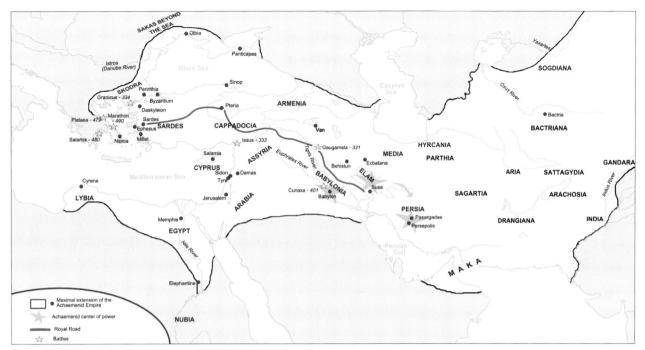

Map of the Royal Road from Shushan to Sardis at the edge of the empire

Existing remains of the Royal Road which connected Shushan to Sardis and which was used by the king's swift riders. Herodotus describes this road in detail.

southwest, and some roads reached the eastern corners of the empire. With the aid of tablets discovered in the Persepolis treasury, it is possible to reconstruct these roads as well.

A few hundred of the Persepolis Fortification tablets which have been published deal with food rations given to the couriers who were carrying royal documents. They provide additional information about the courier system that appears a few times in the Megillah. Not surprisingly, Shushan and Persepolis, the royal citadels, are the cities most commonly mentioned in this group of tablets. Reference is made to documents sent to or received from Shushan and Persepolis, some of which came from or went to the edges of the empire. For example, PF 1318 and 1383 deal with sealed documents sent between Shushan and India (see map above, on *Esther* 1:1). PF 1404 refers to a sealed document being delivered from Sardis to Persepolis. Many (PF 1286, 1308, and 1335, among others) discuss documents that went from Shushan to Persepolis and vice versa. The concept of a fast messenger also appears on some tablets. PF 1285 and 1319 deal with rations for fast messengers carrying sealed documents of the king.

Each tablet has cuneiform writing on one side and various seal impressions on the other. Apparently, the person in charge of dispensing the food would impress his seal into the tablet upon giving the courier his rations, and the courier would impress his seal into the tablet to confirm that he had received them. These tablets would then serve as a receipt for the transaction, authenticated by both parties.

Some of the tablets found seem to have acted as an authorization for the courier to receive food rations along the way from royal storehouses. An interesting stipulation was that the courier was to be given rations per day of travel. Should he spend an extra day in the same place, he was not entitled to additional rations. This was to assure that the messenger would not waste his time along the way.

No doubt, the couriers who delivered the decrees mentioned here in the Megillah had to impress their seals into similar tablets to confirm that they had indeed received their rations.

15 *Mordechai then came out from before the king with royal apparel of aquamarine (t'cheles) and white (chur), a large golden cloak, a fine linen (butz) cloak and a purple [wool cloak] (argaman), and the city of Shushan was jubilant and joyful.*

In order to fully envision the royal garments, let us use a description by the Roman historian, Quintus Curtius Rufus:[50]

> The sumptuous attire of the king was especially remarkable. His tunic was purple with white woven into it at the center, and his gold-embroidered cloak had a gilded motif of hawks attacking each other with their beaks. From his gold belt which he wore in a female way, he had slung his dagger, the scabbard decorated with precious stones. His royal diadem was encircled by a blue ribbon with white flecks.

Clearly, the description of a purple tunic with white woven into the center matches the "fine linen cloak (*butz*) and a purple [wool cloak] (*argaman*)" described here in the Megillah. (In the ancient world, linen could not be dyed and thus was always white.) Apparently, this was actually one garment, not two. In essence, the cloak was *sha'atnez*, a combination of wool and linen, something that is prohibited for Jews to wear. How did Mordechai wear this garment?[51]

....
50. *The Persian Empire*, p. 531.

51. The Brisker Rav asked this question. He proved from *Megillah* 16b that the *butz* and *argaman* formed one cloak.

The answer must be that this garment did not fit the Torah prohibition of *sha'atnez*. According to Rashi (*Nidah* 61b), for example, the Torah prohibition applies only if the wool and linen were combed, spun, and woven together. If the two materials were woven together but not spun together, the prohibition to wear this garment would be *mi-d'Rabanan*. In the case of Mordechai, he was permitted to wear *sha'atnez mi-d'Rabanan* for the sake of peace with the king (*sh'lom malchus*).

The gold-embroidered cloak mentioned by Curtius Rufus corresponds to the "large golden cloak" given to Mordechai. The royal diadem was a special cloth that each Persian king wore around his head. Another Roman historian describes the royal diadem that Alexander the Great took from the last Persian king (Darius III); it was long enough to encircle his head with the ends reaching down to his shoulders and was surrounded by a blue ribbon with white flecks. These descriptions seem to match the "royal apparel of aquamarine (*t'cheles*) and white (*chur*)" mentioned here in the Megillah. The "royal apparel" refers to the royal diadem; the "*t'cheles*" was wool dyed blue and the "*chur*" was white. According to this, the *t'cheles* that Mordechai wore may have been a blue ribbon, not a blue garment. This would be similar to the blue ribbon of *t'cheles* that the *Kohen Gadol* wore on his head to hold up the *tzitz*.

A Persepolis relief depicting the Persian king dressed in the royal garments, flanked by two attendants

ESTHER 9

7...And Parshandasa and Dalfon and Aspasa.

Left: A cylinder seal from the Persian period, written in Aramaic, which carries the name Parshandasa son of Arsadasan. Parshandasa may have been a common Persian name. Right: A modern impression created using this seal. (Photographs reproduced by kind permission of the Trustees of the British Museum)

19 Therefore do the Jews of the villages, that dwell in the unwalled towns, make the fourteenth day of the month Adar a day of gladness and feasting, and a good day, and of sending portions one to another.

"Mishloach Manos": A Persepolis relief showing servants bringing foods to the king's table. Similar motifs made from colored glazed bricks adorned the walls of the palace in Shushan, as is evident from the designs found on some bricks discovered there.

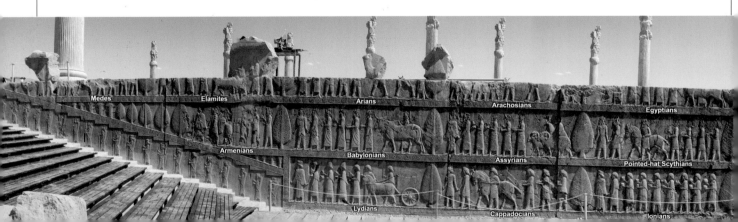

1 *King Achashverosh then imposed a tax, [both] on the mainland and the sea islands.*

Running and controlling this vast empire was of course dependent on the ability to collect and raise taxes. The Persians had worked this out to perfection. Herodotus describes the tax system in detail, listing the amount each satrapy was required to bring to the king's treasury per annum. There are Persepolis reliefs showing some of the various nations presenting their annual tax to the king. One may ask why the Megillah stresses here that Achashverosh put a tax on the land, when surely taxes were nothing new. The *Targum Sheini* learns from this verse that he exempted the Jewish people from taxes in honor of Esther, while laying taxes upon the other countries. When Esther first became queen, the king honored her by lowering taxes everywhere (*Esther* 2:18). The king would have just exempted Esther's nation from taxes entirely, but he did not know her nationality at the time. He therefore lowered the taxes on all of the nations. Now, upon discovering Esther's origin, Achashverosh exempted her nation from taxes and restored the original tax upon all other nations. This understanding fits with our knowledge of the Persian

Set of reliefs from the wall of the Persepolis *apadna*, showing various nations bringing their annual tribute to the king. The scenes are separated from each other by trees. The people in each scene are dressed differently, representing different lands or nations. Each group is led by a Persian or Median official on an alternating basis. Each nation presented the land's pride and joy to the king. Based on Persian lists we have a fairly good idea of which countries and nations are represented here, although scholars differ on the exact identity of each ethnic group shown. The verse states that the taxes were levied upon the lands and islands. The Ionians, for example, were the Greeks who lived on islands. Other nations lived on mainlands.

tax system: Herodotus relates that all nations were taxed except for the Persian nation; as rulers of the empire, they were not required to pay the annual tax. According to the *Targum Sheini*, this special status applied also to the queen's nation, which in this case was the Jewish nation.

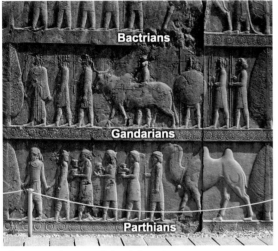
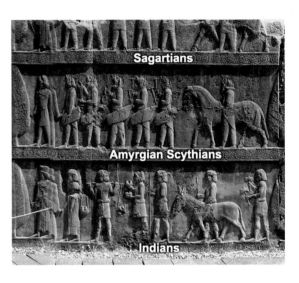

Close-ups of some of the delegations

2 *And the entire account of his power and might, and the details of Mordechai's greatness [to which] the king promoted him, are indeed written in the book of chronicles of the kings of Media and Persia.*

As mentioned earlier, we do not have many surviving historical documents from the Persians. The Megillah tells us here that all of Achashverosh's "power and might" was documented in the king's chronicles. (This sort of epilogue is commonly found in the Tanach when summing up the history of kings.) Unfortunately, none of these chronicles have been found.

Epilogue

After the Megillah

According to the Gemara (*Megillah* 11b), Achashverosh died shortly after the story of Megillas Esther. It seems from both *Targum* (*Esther* 1:1) and *Targum Sheini* (ibid.) that his death was untimely. Likewise, a cuneiform tablet was found which states that King Xerxes was assassinated, perhaps by his own son.

The Persian kings from that time period were buried at a site known today as Naksh-i-Rustam,

Cuneiform tablet referring to the assassination of Xerxes (photograph reproduced by kind permission of the Trustees of the British Museum)

not far from Persepolis. There are four elaborate tombs carved into the rock face. However, only the tomb of Darius, Xerxes' father, has a name inscribed on it. The inscription is accompanied by a relief which depicts the king standing on a dais, paying tribute to his god. The dais is supported by figures representing the prominent nations of the empire. In the text, Darius describes in detail the empire he established. He points out that one who sees this dais will know

how far the Persian spear and bow have traveled.

No inscriptions whatsoever were found on the other tombs. Because the royal tombs were looted in antiquity, no bones or artifacts have been discovered in any of the tombs either. It is believed that the tomb of Xerxes is one of those adjacent to Darius' tomb.

Artaxerxes

According to conventional history, the king succeeding Xerxes was his son Artaxerxes. He is referred to in *Ezra* by the names Daryavesh, Artachshaste, and Coresh. He acted favorably toward the Jews and permitted them to rebuild the Beis Hamikdash and surround Jerusalem with a city wall. During his reign, Ezra and Nechemiah returned to Eretz Yisrael from Babylon and Shushan; they became the leaders of the Jewish people who were there. All of this is described in the Books of *Ezra* (from Chapter 7 and on) and *Nechemiah*.

Mordechai and Esther

What became of Mordechai and Esther after the story of Megillas Esther? Esther had no choice but to remain in the palace of Achashverosh. According to some traditions, Mordechai moved back to Eretz Yisrael after the building of the Second Beis Hamikdash. Nonetheless, the Jews of Persia had a tradition that Mordechai and Esther are buried in the city of Hamadan, which was the original capital of Media. The custom to visit their graves before Purim continues until this very day.

Three of the four royal tombs carved into the rock at Naksh-i-Rustam (the fourth tomb is off to the right and does not appear in the picture). The right tomb shown here is that of Darius. Xerxes was buried either in the center tomb or in the tomb not shown here.

The tomb of Darius. Here the king is seen standing on a dais, paying tribute to his god. The figures underneath are meant to represent the prominent nations of the empire. The framed area contains text attesting to the fact that it is Darius' tomb.

The building in
Hamadan which
houses the tombs of
Mordechai and Esther

The tombs of
Mordechai and
Esther in Hamadan

Bibliography

Bleiberg, E. *Jewish Life in Ancient Egypt: A Family Archive from the Nile Valley.* Brooklyn: Brooklyn Museum of Art, 2002.

Boucharlat, R. "Susa under Achaemenid Rule." In *Mesopotamia and Iran in the Persian Period.* London: British Museum Press, 1997, pp. 54-67.

Bowman, R. A. "Aramaic Ritual Texts from Persepolis." *Oriental Institute Publications* 91 (1970).

Chefetz, C. *Malchut Paras biTekufat Bayit Sheini v'Lifanehah: Iyun Mechudash. Megadim* (14), pp. 78-147.

Curtis, J. "The Archaeology of the Achaemenid Period." In Curtis, J., and N. Tallis (eds.). *Forgotten Empire: The World of Ancient Persia.* London: British Museum Press, 2005, pp. 30-49.

Curtis, J., and S. Razmjou. "The Palace." In Curtis, J., and N. Tallis (eds.). *Forgotten Empire: The World of Ancient Persia.* London: British Museum Press, 2005, pp. 50-103.

Curtis, J., and N. Tallis (eds.). *Forgotten Empire: The World of Ancient Persia.* London: British Museum Press, 2005.

Danziger, Rabbi S. E. "Who Was the Real Akhashverosh." *The Jewish Observer* (Feb 1973), pp. 12-15.

First, M. *Jewish History in Conflict.* Northvale, NJ: Jason Aronson, 1997.

Harper, Prudence O., J. Aruz, and F. Talon (eds.). *The Royal City of Susa: Ancient Near Eastern Treasures in the Louvre.* New York: Metropolitan Museum of Art, 1992.

Kaptan, D. *The Daskyleion Bullae: Seal images from the Western Achaemenid Empire* (2 vols.). Leiden: The Netherlands Institute for the Near East, 2002.

Krefter, F. *Persepolis Rekonstructionen.* Berlin: Gebruder Mann Verlag, 1971.

Kuhrt, A. *The Persian Empire.* New York: Routledge, 2007.

Perrot, J., and D. Ladiray. "The Palace of Susa." In Goodnick Westenholz, Joan (ed.). *Royal Cities of the Biblical World.* Jerusalem: Bible Lands Museum, 1996, pp. 236-254.

Pritchard, James B. (ed.). *Ancient Near Eastern Texts: Relating to the Old Testament.* Princeton: Princeton University Press, 1969.

Rabinowitz, Rabbi Y.E. Halevi. *Dorot HaRishonim, Tekufat Hamikra.* Jerusalem: Dr. B.M. Levin, 1939.

Schmidt, E. F. "Persepolis II: Contents of the Treasury and Other Discoveries." *Oriental Institute Publications* 69 (1957).

Simpson, St. J. "The Royal Table." In Curtis, J., and N. Tallis (eds.). *Forgotten Empire: The World of Ancient Persia.* London: British Museum Press, 2005, pp. 104-131.

Tallis, N. "Transport and Warfare." In Curtis, J., and N. Tallis (eds.). *Forgotten Empire: The World of Ancient Persia.* London: British Museum Press, 2005, pp.210-217.

Yamauchi, Edwin M. *Persia And the Bible.* Grand Rapids: Baker Books, 1990, 1996.

———. "The Archaeological Background of Esther." *Bibliotheca Sacra* (April June 1980), pp. 99-117.

כָּכָה וּמָה הִגִּיעַ אֲלֵיהֶם: כז קִיְּמוּ וקבל כתיב
וְקִבֵּל הַיְּהוּדִים | עֲלֵיהֶם | וְעַל־זַרְעָם וְעַל כָּל־
הַנִּלְוִים עֲלֵיהֶם וְלֹא יַעֲבוֹר לִהְיוֹת עֹשִׂים אֵת
שְׁנֵי הַיָּמִים הָאֵלֶּה כִּכְתָבָם וְכִזְמַנָּם בְּכָל־שָׁנָה
וְשָׁנָה: כח וְהַיָּמִים הָאֵלֶּה נִזְכָּרִים וְנַעֲשִׂים בְּכָל־
דּוֹר וָדוֹר מִשְׁפָּחָה וּמִשְׁפָּחָה מְדִינָה וּמְדִינָה
וְעִיר וָעִיר וִימֵי הַפּוּרִים הָאֵלֶּה לֹא יַעַבְרוּ
מִתּוֹךְ הַיְּהוּדִים וְזִכְרָם לֹא־יָסוּף מִזַּרְעָם:

כט וַתִּכְתֹּב אֶסְתֵּר הַמַּלְכָּה בַת־אֲבִיחַיִל
וּמָרְדֳּכַי הַיְּהוּדִי אֶת־כָּל־תֹּקֶף לְקַיֵּם אֵת
אִגֶּרֶת הַפֻּרִים הַזֹּאת הַשֵּׁנִית: ל וַיִּשְׁלַח סְפָרִים
אֶל־כָּל־הַיְּהוּדִים אֶל־שֶׁבַע וְעֶשְׂרִים וּמֵאָה
מְדִינָה מַלְכוּת אֲחַשְׁוֵרוֹשׁ דִּבְרֵי שָׁלוֹם וֶאֱמֶת:
לא לְקַיֵּם אֶת־יְמֵי הַפֻּרִים הָאֵלֶּה בִּזְמַנֵּיהֶם
כַּאֲשֶׁר קִיַּם עֲלֵיהֶם מָרְדֳּכַי הַיְּהוּדִי וְאֶסְתֵּר
הַמַּלְכָּה וְכַאֲשֶׁר קִיְּמוּ עַל־נַפְשָׁם וְעַל־זַרְעָם
דִּבְרֵי הַצֹּמוֹת וְזַעֲקָתָם: לב וּמַאֲמַר אֶסְתֵּר קִיַּם
דִּבְרֵי הַפֻּרִים הָאֵלֶּה וְנִכְתָּב בַּסֵּפֶר:

פרק י

א וַיָּשֶׂם הַמֶּלֶךְ אחשרש כתיב אֲחַשְׁוֵרֹשׁ | מַס עַל־
הָאָרֶץ וְאִיֵּי הַיָּם: ב וְכָל־מַעֲשֵׂה תָקְפּוֹ וּגְבוּרָתוֹ
וּפָרָשַׁת גְּדֻלַּת מָרְדֳּכַי אֲשֶׁר גִּדְּלוֹ הַמֶּלֶךְ
הֲלוֹא־הֵם כְּתוּבִים עַל־סֵפֶר דִּבְרֵי הַיָּמִים
לְמַלְכֵי מָדַי וּפָרָס: ג כִּי | מָרְדֳּכַי הַיְּהוּדִי מִשְׁנֶה
לַמֶּלֶךְ אֲחַשְׁוֵרוֹשׁ וְגָדוֹל לַיְּהוּדִים וְרָצוּי לְרֹב
אֶחָיו דֹּרֵשׁ טוֹב לְעַמּוֹ וְדֹבֵר שָׁלוֹם לְכָל־זַרְעוֹ:

observed in every generation, every family, every state and every city; and [that] these days of Purim shall not disappear from among the Jews, and their commemoration shall not cease from [among] their descendants.

[29] Queen Esther, the daughter of Avichayil, with Mordechai the Jew, wrote down the magnitude of all [the miracles], so as to establish this second letter of Purim. [30] [Mordechai] then sent letters to all the Jews — to the hundred and twenty-seven states, the kingdom of Achashverosh — [with] words of peace and truth, [31] in order to establish these days of Purim at their [prescribed] times, just as Mordechai the Jew and Queen Esther had instituted for them, and just as they had taken upon themselves and their descendants, [as well as] the fasts and their prayers. [32] And [through] Esther's petition, these words of [the letter of] Purim were established and written in the book [of Holy Writings].

Chapter 10

King Achashverosh then imposed a tax, [both] on the mainland and the sea islands. [2] And the entire account of his power and might, and the details of Mordechai's greatness [to which] the king promoted him, are indeed written in the book of chronicles of the kings of Media and Persia. [3] For Mordechai the Jew was King Achashverosh's viceroy, the leader of the Jews, and accepted by most of his brethren, promoting his people's welfare and preaching peace for all their descendants.

and joy. [19] Therefore, the rural Jews who live in the open towns observe the fourteenth day of the month of Adar as [a day of] joy and feasting and a holiday, with the sending of food gifts, each to his friend. [20] Mordechai wrote down these events, and sent letters to all the Jews in all the states of King Achashverosh, those near and far, [21] [for them] to take upon themselves to observe each year the fourteenth day of the month of Adar and the fifteenth, [22] like the days on which the Jews rested from [fighting] their enemies, and [in] the month that was transformed for them from misery to joy, and from mourning to a holiday; [for the Jews] to observe them as days of feasting and joy, with the sending of food gifts, each to his friend, and donations to the needy. [23] The Jews [unanimously] accepted upon themselves that which they had begun to observe, and [those laws] which Mordechai had written for them [to keep]. [24] For Haman the son of Hamedasa, the Agagi, the oppressor of all the Jews, devised [a plan] against the Jews to annihilate them, and cast *pur*, which is the lot, to throw them into confusion and to annihilate them. [25] But when [Esther] came before the king [and entreated him, the king] said, with [his words being written down as] bills of law, [that Haman's] evil plan which he devised against the Jews be reversed [to fall] upon his [own] head, and they hanged him and his sons on the gallows. [26] Therefore, they called these days Purim on account of the *pur*. [To publicize] this, all the words of this letter [were written], and [to tell] what prompted [these people to act] this way, and what [subsequently] happened to them. [27] The Jews took and accepted upon themselves and their descendants, and upon all those who join them — and it must not be transgressed — to observe these two days; [and that the scroll be written] according to its [prescribed form of] script; and [that the days be observed] at their [proper] time each year; [28] and [that] these days [be] commemorated and

וְשִׁבְעִים אֶ֔לֶף וּבַ֨בִּזָּ֔ה לֹ֥א שָׁלְח֖וּ אֶת־יָדָֽם׃ יז בְּיוֹם־שְׁלוֹשָׁ֨ה עָשָׂ֜ר לְחֹ֣דֶשׁ אֲדָ֗ר וְנ֛וֹחַ בְּאַרְבָּעָ֥ה עָשָׂ֖ר בּ֑וֹ וְעָשֹׂ֣ה אֹת֔וֹ י֖וֹם מִשְׁתֶּ֥ה וְשִׂמְחָֽה׃ יח וְהַיְּהוּדִ֣ים כתיב וְהַיְּהוּדִ֣ים אֲשֶׁר־בְּשׁוּשָׁ֗ן נִקְהֲלוּ֙ בִּשְׁלוֹשָׁ֤ה עָשָׂר֙ בּ֔וֹ וּבְאַרְבָּעָ֥ה עָשָׂ֖ר בּ֑וֹ וְנ֗וֹחַ בַּחֲמִשָּׁ֤ה עָשָׂר֙ בּ֔וֹ וְעָשֹׂ֣ה אֹת֔וֹ י֖וֹם מִשְׁתֶּ֥ה וְשִׂמְחָֽה׃ יט עַל־כֵּ֞ן הַיְּהוּדִ֣ים הַפְּרֹזִים֙ כתיב הַפְּרָזִ֗ים הַיֹּשְׁבִים֙ בְּעָרֵ֣י הַפְּרָז֔וֹת עֹשִׂ֗ים אֵ֠ת י֣וֹם אַרְבָּעָ֨ה עָשָׂ֥ר לְחֹ֣דֶשׁ אֲדָ֗ר שִׂמְחָ֤ה וּמִשְׁתֶּה֙ וְי֣וֹם ט֔וֹב וּמִשְׁלֹ֥חַ מָנ֖וֹת אִ֥ישׁ לְרֵעֵֽהוּ׃ כ וַיִּכְתֹּ֣ב מָרְדֳּכַ֔י אֶת־הַדְּבָרִ֖ים הָאֵ֑לֶּה וַיִּשְׁלַ֣ח סְפָרִ֗ים אֶל־כָּל־הַיְּהוּדִ֞ים אֲשֶׁר֙ בְּכָל־מְדִינוֹת֙ הַמֶּ֣לֶךְ אֲחַשְׁוֵר֔וֹשׁ הַקְּרוֹבִ֖ים וְהָרְחוֹקִֽים׃ כא לְקַיֵּם֙ עֲלֵיהֶ֔ם לִהְי֣וֹת עֹשִׂ֗ים אֵ֠ת י֣וֹם אַרְבָּעָ֨ה עָשָׂ֥ר לְחֹ֣דֶשׁ אֲדָ֛ר וְאֵ֥ת יוֹם־חֲמִשָּׁ֥ה עָשָׂ֖ר בּ֑וֹ בְּכָל־שָׁנָ֖ה וְשָׁנָֽה׃ כב כַּיָּמִ֗ים אֲשֶׁר־נָ֨חוּ בָהֶ֤ם הַיְּהוּדִים֙ מֵאֹ֣יְבֵיהֶ֔ם וְהַחֹ֗דֶשׁ אֲשֶׁר֩ נֶהְפַּ֨ךְ לָהֶ֤ם מִיָּגוֹן֙ לְשִׂמְחָ֔ה וּמֵאֵ֖בֶל לְי֣וֹם ט֑וֹב לַעֲשׂ֣וֹת אוֹתָ֗ם יְמֵי֙ מִשְׁתֶּ֣ה וְשִׂמְחָ֔ה וּמִשְׁלֹ֤חַ מָנוֹת֙ אִ֣ישׁ לְרֵעֵ֔הוּ וּמַתָּנ֖וֹת לָֽאֶבְיֹנִֽים׃ כג וְקִבֵּל֙ הַיְּהוּדִ֔ים אֵ֥ת אֲשֶׁר־הֵחֵ֖לּוּ לַעֲשׂ֑וֹת וְאֵ֛ת אֲשֶׁר־כָּתַ֥ב מָרְדֳּכַ֖י אֲלֵיהֶֽם׃ כד כִּי֩ הָמָ֨ן בֶּֽן־הַמְּדָ֜תָא הָֽאֲגָגִ֗י צֹרֵר֙ כָּל־הַיְּהוּדִ֔ים חָשַׁ֥ב עַל־הַיְּהוּדִ֖ים לְאַבְּדָ֑ם וְהִפִּ֥יל פּוּר֙ ה֣וּא הַגּוֹרָ֔ל לְהֻמָּ֖ם וּֽלְאַבְּדָֽם׃ כה וּבְבֹאָהּ֮ לִפְנֵ֣י הַמֶּלֶךְ֒ אָמַ֣ר עִם־הַסֵּ֔פֶר יָשׁ֞וּב מַחֲשַׁבְתּ֧וֹ הָרָעָ֛ה אֲשֶׁר־חָשַׁ֥ב עַל־הַיְּהוּדִ֖ים עַל־רֹאשׁ֑וֹ וְתָל֥וּ אֹת֛וֹ וְאֶת־בָּנָ֖יו עַל־הָעֵֽץ׃ כו עַל־כֵּ֡ן קָֽרְא֣וּ לַיָּמִ֣ים הָ֠אֵלֶּה פוּרִים֮ עַל־שֵׁ֣ם הַפּוּר֒ עַל־כֵּ֕ן עַל־כָּל־דִּבְרֵ֖י הָאִגֶּ֣רֶת הַזֹּ֑את וּמָֽה־רָא֣וּ עַל־

וְהַפַּחוֹת וְעֹשֵׂי הַמְּלָאכָה אֲשֶׁר לַמֶּלֶךְ
מְנַשְּׂאִים אֶת־הַיְּהוּדִים כִּי־נָפַל פַּחַד־מָרְדֳּכַי
עֲלֵיהֶם: ד כִּי־גָדוֹל מָרְדֳּכַי בְּבֵית הַמֶּלֶךְ
וְשָׁמְעוֹ הוֹלֵךְ בְּכָל־הַמְּדִינוֹת כִּי־הָאִישׁ
מָרְדֳּכַי הוֹלֵךְ וְגָדוֹל: ה וַיַּכּוּ הַיְּהוּדִים בְּכָל־
אֹיְבֵיהֶם מַכַּת־חֶרֶב וְהֶרֶג וְאַבְדָן וַיַּעֲשׂוּ
בְשֹׂנְאֵיהֶם כִּרְצוֹנָם: ו וּבְשׁוּשַׁן הַבִּירָה הָרְגוּ
הַיְּהוּדִים וְאַבֵּד חֲמֵשׁ מֵאוֹת אִישׁ: ז וְאֵת |
פַּרְשַׁנְדָּתָא וְאֵת | דַּלְפוֹן וְאֵת | אַסְפָּתָא:
ח וְאֵת | פּוֹרָתָא וְאֵת | אֲדַלְיָא וְאֵת |
אֲרִידָתָא: ט וְאֵת | פַּרְמַשְׁתָּא וְאֵת | אֲרִיסַי
וְאֵת | אֲרִדַי וְאֵת | וַיְזָתָא: י עֲשֶׂרֶת בְּנֵי הָמָן
בֶּן־הַמְּדָתָא צֹרֵר הַיְּהוּדִים הָרָגוּ וּבַבִּזָּה לֹא
שָׁלְחוּ אֶת־יָדָם: יא בַּיּוֹם הַהוּא בָּא מִסְפַּר
הַהֲרוּגִים בְּשׁוּשַׁן הַבִּירָה לִפְנֵי הַמֶּלֶךְ:
יב וַיֹּאמֶר הַמֶּלֶךְ לְאֶסְתֵּר הַמַּלְכָּה בְּשׁוּשַׁן
הַבִּירָה הָרְגוּ הַיְּהוּדִים וְאַבֵּד חֲמֵשׁ מֵאוֹת
אִישׁ וְאֵת עֲשֶׂרֶת בְּנֵי־הָמָן בִּשְׁאָר מְדִינוֹת
הַמֶּלֶךְ מֶה עָשׂוּ וּמַה־שְּׁאֵלָתֵךְ וְיִנָּתֵן לָךְ וּמַה־
בַּקָּשָׁתֵךְ עוֹד וְתֵעָשׂ: יג וַתֹּאמֶר אֶסְתֵּר אִם־
עַל־הַמֶּלֶךְ טוֹב יִנָּתֵן גַּם־מָחָר לַיְּהוּדִים אֲשֶׁר
בְּשׁוּשָׁן לַעֲשׂוֹת כְּדָת הַיּוֹם וְאֵת עֲשֶׂרֶת
בְּנֵי־הָמָן יִתְלוּ עַל־הָעֵץ: יד וַיֹּאמֶר הַמֶּלֶךְ
לְהֵעָשׂוֹת כֵּן וַתִּנָּתֵן דָּת בְּשׁוּשָׁן וְאֵת עֲשֶׂרֶת
בְּנֵי־הָמָן תָּלוּ: טו וַיִּקָּהֲלוּ הַיְּהוּדִים הַיְּהוּדִים כתיב
אֲשֶׁר־בְּשׁוּשַׁן גַּם בְּיוֹם אַרְבָּעָה עָשָׂר לְחֹדֶשׁ
אֲדָר וַיַּהַרְגוּ בְשׁוּשָׁן שְׁלֹשׁ מֵאוֹת אִישׁ וּבַבִּזָּה
לֹא שָׁלְחוּ אֶת־יָדָם: טז וּשְׁאָר הַיְּהוּדִים אֲשֶׁר
בִּמְדִינוֹת הַמֶּלֶךְ נִקְהֲלוּ | וְעָמֹד עַל־נַפְשָׁם
וְנוֹחַ מֵאֹיְבֵיהֶם וְהָרֹג בְּשֹׂנְאֵיהֶם חֲמִשָּׁה

king's household and his fame spread throughout the states, because the [great] man, Mordechai, was steadily becoming greater. ⁵ The Jews smote their enemies with the sword and [other forms of] killing and extermination, and did as they wished to those who hated them. ⁶ And in the citadel of Shushan the Jews killed and annihilated five hundred men. ⁷And Parshandasa and Dalfon and Aspasa, ⁸ and Porasa and Adalya and Aridasa, ⁹ and Parmashta and Arisai and Aridai and Vaizasa, ¹⁰the ten sons of Haman the son of Hamedasa, the oppressor of the Jews, they killed, but they did not lay their hands on [any of] the booty. ¹¹ On that day, the number of those killed in the citadel of Shushan came before the king. ¹²The king then said to Queen Esther, "In Shushan the capital the Jews killed and annihilated five hundred men and the ten sons of Haman. In the other states of the king what did they do? And what is your request and it will be granted you? And what further wish do you have and it will be done?" ¹³ Esther answered, "If it pleases the king, let tomorrow, as well, be given for the Jews in Shushan to act according to the law [that applied] today, and let them hang the ten sons of Haman on the gallows." ¹⁴The king declared that this be done and it was made law in Shushan, and the ten sons of Haman they hanged. ¹⁵The Jews in Shushan grouped together also on the fourteenth of the month of Adar and killed three hundred men in Shushan, but they did not lay their hands on [any of] the booty. ¹⁶ And the rest of the Jews in the [other] states of the king grouped together, protecting their lives, and were relieved of their enemies and killed seventy-five thousand of those who hated them, but they did not lay their hands on [any of] the booty. ¹⁷ [This was] on the thirteenth of the month of Adar, and they rested on the fourteenth, making it a day of feasting and joy. ¹⁸ But the Jews in Shushan grouped together on the thirteenth and fourteenth of [the month], and rested on the fifteenth, making it a day of feasting

וּלְאַבֵּד אֶת־כָּל־חֵיל עַם וּמְדִינָה הַצָּרִים
אֹתָם טַף וְנָשִׁים וּשְׁלָלָם לָבוֹז: יג בְּיוֹם אֶחָד
בְּכָל־מְדִינוֹת הַמֶּלֶךְ אֲחַשְׁוֵרוֹשׁ בִּשְׁלוֹשָׁה
עָשָׂר לְחֹדֶשׁ שְׁנֵים־עָשָׂר הוּא־חֹדֶשׁ אֲדָר:
יג פַּתְשֶׁגֶן הַכְּתָב לְהִנָּתֵן דָּת בְּכָל־מְדִינָה
וּמְדִינָה גָּלוּי לְכָל־הָעַמִּים וְלִהְיוֹת היהודיים
כְּתִיב הַיְּהוּדִים עתודים כְּתִיב עֲתִידִים לַיּוֹם הַזֶּה
לְהִנָּקֵם מֵאֹיְבֵיהֶם: יד הָרָצִים רֹכְבֵי הָרֶכֶשׁ
הָאֲחַשְׁתְּרָנִים יָצְאוּ מְבֹהָלִים וּדְחוּפִים בִּדְבַר
הַמֶּלֶךְ וְהַדָּת נִתְּנָה בְּשׁוּשַׁן הַבִּירָה:

טו וּמָרְדֳּכַי יָצָא | מִלִּפְנֵי הַמֶּלֶךְ בִּלְבוּשׁ מַלְכוּת
תְּכֵלֶת וָחוּר וַעֲטֶרֶת זָהָב גְּדוֹלָה וְתַכְרִיךְ
בּוּץ וְאַרְגָּמָן וְהָעִיר שׁוּשָׁן צָהֲלָה וְשָׂמֵחָה:
טז לַיְּהוּדִים הָיְתָה אוֹרָה וְשִׂמְחָה וְשָׂשֹׂן וִיקָר:
יז וּבְכָל־מְדִינָה וּמְדִינָה וּבְכָל־עִיר וָעִיר מְקוֹם
אֲשֶׁר דְּבַר־הַמֶּלֶךְ וְדָתוֹ מַגִּיעַ שִׂמְחָה וְשָׂשׂוֹן
לַיְּהוּדִים מִשְׁתֶּה וְיוֹם טוֹב וְרַבִּים מֵעַמֵּי הָאָרֶץ
מִתְיַהֲדִים כִּי־נָפַל פַּחַד־הַיְּהוּדִים עֲלֵיהֶם:

פרק ט

א וּבִשְׁנֵים עָשָׂר חֹדֶשׁ הוּא־חֹדֶשׁ אֲדָר
בִּשְׁלוֹשָׁה עָשָׂר יוֹם בּוֹ אֲשֶׁר הִגִּיעַ דְּבַר־
הַמֶּלֶךְ וְדָתוֹ לְהֵעָשׂוֹת בַּיּוֹם אֲשֶׁר שִׂבְּרוּ אֹיְבֵי
הַיְּהוּדִים לִשְׁלוֹט בָּהֶם וְנַהֲפוֹךְ הוּא אֲשֶׁר
יִשְׁלְטוּ הַיְּהוּדִים הֵמָּה בְּשֹׂנְאֵיהֶם: ב נִקְהֲלוּ
הַיְּהוּדִים בְּעָרֵיהֶם בְּכָל־מְדִינוֹת הַמֶּלֶךְ
אֲחַשְׁוֵרוֹשׁ לִשְׁלֹחַ יָד בִּמְבַקְשֵׁי רָעָתָם וְאִישׁ
לֹא־עָמַד לִפְנֵיהֶם כִּי־נָפַל פַּחְדָּם עַל־כָּל־
הָעַמִּים: ג וְכָל־שָׂרֵי הַמְּדִינוֹת וְהָאֲחַשְׁדַּרְפְּנִים

---

twelfth month, the month of Adar. [13] The text of the document was to become law in every state, publicized for all the nations, and for the Jews to be prepared for this day to avenge themselves of their enemies. [14] The swift riders, the riders of the king's elite express camels, set out in a rush and hurry with the king's decree, and the law was published in the citadel of Shushan.

[15] Mordechai then came out from before the king with royal apparel of aquamarine (*t'cheles*) and white (*chur*), a large golden cloak, a fine linen (*butz*) cloak and a purple [wool cloak] (*argaman*), and the city of Shushan was jubilant and joyful. [16] For the Jews there was [then] enlightenment, joy, elation and honor. [17] And in every state and every city — wherever the king's decree reached and his law [took effect — there was] joy and elation for the Jews, [with] feasting and a holiday; and many of the common people converted to Judaism, for they were afraid of the Jews.

Chapter 9

And in the twelfth month, the month of Adar, on the thirteenth day of [the month], when [the time] came for the king's decree and law to be carried out — on the day the enemies of the Jews had hoped to gain power over them, but [the situation] was reversed, that the Jews could [now] gain power over their enemies — [2] the Jews grouped together in their cities, in all the states of King Achashverosh, to act against those who sought them harm, but no man [even] stood in their way, for all the nations were afraid of them. [3] And the state ministers, satraps and governors, and the administrators of the king's affairs raised the status of the Jews, since they were afraid of Mordechai. [4] For Mordechai was esteemed in the

עַל־הַיְּהוּדִים: וַיּוֹשֶׁט הַמֶּלֶךְ לְאֶסְתֵּר אֵת
שַׁרְבִט הַזָּהָב וַתָּקָם אֶסְתֵּר וַתַּעֲמֹד לִפְנֵי
הַמֶּלֶךְ: וַתֹּאמֶר אִם־עַל־הַמֶּלֶךְ טוֹב וְאִם־
מָצָאתִי חֵן לְפָנָיו וְכָשֵׁר הַדָּבָר לִפְנֵי הַמֶּלֶךְ
וְטוֹבָה אֲנִי בְּעֵינָיו יִכָּתֵב לְהָשִׁיב אֶת־
הַסְּפָרִים מַחֲשֶׁבֶת הָמָן בֶּן־הַמְּדָתָא הָאֲגָגִי
אֲשֶׁר כָּתַב לְאַבֵּד אֶת־הַיְּהוּדִים אֲשֶׁר בְּכָל־
מְדִינוֹת הַמֶּלֶךְ: כִּי אֵיכָכָה אוּכַל וְרָאִיתִי
בָּרָעָה אֲשֶׁר־יִמְצָא אֶת־עַמִּי וְאֵיכָכָה אוּכַל
וְרָאִיתִי בְּאָבְדַן מוֹלַדְתִּי:

וַיֹּאמֶר הַמֶּלֶךְ אֲחַשְׁוֵרוֹשׁ לְאֶסְתֵּר הַמַּלְכָּה
וּלְמָרְדֳּכַי הַיְּהוּדִי הִנֵּה בֵית־הָמָן נָתַתִּי
לְאֶסְתֵּר וְאֹתוֹ תָּלוּ עַל־הָעֵץ עַל אֲשֶׁר־שָׁלַח
יָדוֹ בַּיְּהוּדִים ביהודיים כתיב: וְאַתֶּם כִּתְבוּ
עַל־הַיְּהוּדִים כַּטּוֹב בְּעֵינֵיכֶם בְּשֵׁם הַמֶּלֶךְ
וְחִתְמוּ בְּטַבַּעַת הַמֶּלֶךְ כִּי־כְתָב אֲשֶׁר־
נִכְתָּב בְּשֵׁם־הַמֶּלֶךְ וְנַחְתּוֹם בְּטַבַּעַת הַמֶּלֶךְ
אֵין לְהָשִׁיב: וַיִּקָּרְאוּ סֹפְרֵי הַמֶּלֶךְ בָּעֵת־
הַהִיא בַּחֹדֶשׁ הַשְּׁלִישִׁי הוּא־חֹדֶשׁ סִיוָן
בִּשְׁלוֹשָׁה וְעֶשְׂרִים בּוֹ וַיִּכָּתֵב כְּכָל־אֲשֶׁר־צִוָּה
מָרְדֳּכַי אֶל־הַיְּהוּדִים וְאֶל הָאֲחַשְׁדַּרְפְּנִים
וְהַפַּחוֹת וְשָׂרֵי הַמְּדִינוֹת אֲשֶׁר | מֵהֹדּוּ וְעַד־
כּוּשׁ שֶׁבַע וְעֶשְׂרִים וּמֵאָה מְדִינָה מְדִינָה
וּמְדִינָה כִּכְתָבָהּ וְעַם וָעָם כִּלְשֹׁנוֹ וְאֶל־
הַיְּהוּדִים כִּכְתָבָם וְכִלְשׁוֹנָם: וַיִּכְתֹּב בְּשֵׁם
הַמֶּלֶךְ אֲחַשְׁוֵרֹשׁ וַיַּחְתֹּם בְּטַבַּעַת הַמֶּלֶךְ
וַיִּשְׁלַח סְפָרִים בְּיַד הָרָצִים בַּסּוּסִים רֹכְבֵי
הָרֶכֶשׁ הָאֲחַשְׁתְּרָנִים בְּנֵי הָרַמָּכִים: אֲשֶׁר |
נָתַן הַמֶּלֶךְ לַיְּהוּדִים | אֲשֶׁר בְּכָל־עִיר־וָעִיר
לְהִקָּהֵל וְלַעֲמֹד עַל־נַפְשָׁם לְהַשְׁמִיד וְלַהֲרֹג

to Esther, and Esther arose and stood before the king. [5] She then said, "If it pleases the king and the king regards me favorably, and [if] the king approves of the matter and I am pleasing to him, let it be written to recall the bills [of law], the plan of Haman the son of Hamedasa, the Agagi, that he wrote to annihilate [all] the Jews who are in all the king's states. [6] For how can I witness the misfortune that will befall my people, and how can I witness the annihilation of my kin?!"

[7] King Achashverosh then said to Queen Esther and to Mordechai the Jew, "I have indeed given Haman's estate to Esther, and him they hanged on the gallows because he acted against the Jews. [8] So you, write in the name of the king as you see fit concerning the Jews, and seal [it] with the king's signet ring, for a document that was written in the name of the king and firmly sealed with the king's signet ring cannot be recalled." [9] At that time, in the third month, the month of Sivan, on the twenty-third of [the month], the king's scribes were summoned, and whatever Mordechai ordered concerning the Jews, and concerning the satraps, governors and ministers of the states that extended from Hodu to Cush — one hundred and twenty-seven states — was written down; [to] each state according to its [form of] script, and [to] each nation according to its language; and to the Jews, [as well,] according to their [form of] script and language. [10] [Mordechai] had [all this] written in the name of the king, and sealed [it] with the king's signet ring. He then sent out bills [of law] with the swift horse riders [and] the riders of the king's elite express camels [and] young ponies, [11] [stating] that the king had allowed the Jews in every city to group together and protect their lives, [and] to destroy, kill and annihilate any army of a people or state that attacks them, [and their] children and women, and to plunder their [property as] spoil; [12] on one day, in all the states of King Achashverosh — on the thirteenth of the

ה וַיֹּאמֶר הַמֶּלֶךְ אֲחַשְׁוֵרוֹשׁ וַיֹּאמֶר לְאֶסְתֵּר הַמַּלְכָּה מִי הוּא זֶה וְאֵי־זֶה הוּא אֲשֶׁר־מְלָאוֹ לִבּוֹ לַעֲשׂוֹת כֵּן: ו וַתֹּאמֶר אֶסְתֵּר אִישׁ צַר וְאוֹיֵב הָמָן הָרָע הַזֶּה וְהָמָן נִבְעַת מִלִּפְנֵי הַמֶּלֶךְ וְהַמַּלְכָּה: ז וְהַמֶּלֶךְ קָם בַּחֲמָתוֹ מִמִּשְׁתֵּה הַיַּיִן אֶל־גִּנַּת הַבִּיתָן וְהָמָן עָמַד לְבַקֵּשׁ עַל־נַפְשׁוֹ מֵאֶסְתֵּר הַמַּלְכָּה כִּי רָאָה כִּי־כָלְתָה אֵלָיו הָרָעָה מֵאֵת הַמֶּלֶךְ: ח וְהַמֶּלֶךְ שָׁב מִגִּנַּת הַבִּיתָן אֶל־בֵּית | מִשְׁתֵּה הַיַּיִן וְהָמָן נֹפֵל עַל־הַמִּטָּה אֲשֶׁר אֶסְתֵּר עָלֶיהָ וַיֹּאמֶר הַמֶּלֶךְ הֲגַם לִכְבּוֹשׁ אֶת־הַמַּלְכָּה עִמִּי בַּבָּיִת הַדָּבָר יָצָא מִפִּי הַמֶּלֶךְ וּפְנֵי הָמָן חָפוּ: ט וַיֹּאמֶר חַרְבוֹנָה אֶחָד מִן־הַסָּרִיסִים לִפְנֵי הַמֶּלֶךְ גַּם הִנֵּה־הָעֵץ אֲשֶׁר־עָשָׂה הָמָן לְמָרְדֳּכַי אֲשֶׁר דִּבֶּר־טוֹב עַל־הַמֶּלֶךְ עֹמֵד בְּבֵית הָמָן גָּבֹהַּ חֲמִשִּׁים אַמָּה וַיֹּאמֶר הַמֶּלֶךְ תְּלֻהוּ עָלָיו: י וַיִּתְלוּ אֶת־הָמָן עַל־הָעֵץ אֲשֶׁר־הֵכִין לְמָרְדֳּכָי וַחֲמַת הַמֶּלֶךְ שָׁכָכָה:

פרק ח

א בַּיּוֹם הַהוּא נָתַן הַמֶּלֶךְ אֲחַשְׁוֵרוֹשׁ לְאֶסְתֵּר הַמַּלְכָּה אֶת־בֵּית הָמָן צֹרֵר הַיְּהוּדִיִּים כתיב הַיְּהוּדִים וּמָרְדֳּכַי בָּא לִפְנֵי הַמֶּלֶךְ כִּי־הִגִּידָה אֶסְתֵּר מַה הוּא־לָהּ: ב וַיָּסַר הַמֶּלֶךְ אֶת־טַבַּעְתּוֹ אֲשֶׁר הֶעֱבִיר מֵהָמָן וַיִּתְּנָהּ לְמָרְדֳּכָי וַתָּשֶׂם אֶסְתֵּר אֶת־מָרְדֳּכַי עַל־בֵּית הָמָן:

ג וַתּוֹסֶף אֶסְתֵּר וַתְּדַבֵּר לִפְנֵי הַמֶּלֶךְ וַתִּפֹּל לִפְנֵי רַגְלָיו וַתֵּבְךְּ וַתִּתְחַנֶּן־לוֹ לְהַעֲבִיר אֶת־רָעַת הָמָן הָאֲגָגִי וְאֵת מַחֲשַׁבְתּוֹ אֲשֶׁר חָשַׁב

---

[5] King Achashverosh then said, [speaking directly] to Queen Esther, "Who is this and where is he, who dared to do this?!" [6] Esther replied, "An oppressor and enemy, this evil Haman!" Haman was then terrified before the king and the queen. [7] The king then got up from the wine feast in a rage, [and went out] to the garden of the *bisan* (orchard), while Haman stood up to plead for his life from Queen Esther, for he realized that the king's bad [feelings] toward him were absolute. [8] The king then returned from the garden orchard to the wine feast chamber, [as] Haman was falling on the couch on which Esther was [lying]. The king said, "Does [he] also [wish] to assault the queen in my presence [here] in the palace?!" The words had [hardly] left the king's mouth and [the king's servants] covered Haman's face. [9] Charvonah, one of the attendants, then said before the king, "Here is also the gallows which Haman made for Mordechai, who told over good things for the king, standing in Haman's house, 50 cubits high!" The king replied, "Hang him on it!" [10] So they hanged Haman on the gallows he had prepared for Mordechai, and the king's anger abated.

Chapter 8

On that day, King Achashverosh gave to Queen Esther the estate of Haman, the oppressor of the Jews, and Mordechai came before the king, for Esther had told [the king] what [relation] he was to her. [2] The king then took off his ring that he had removed from Haman, and gave it to Mordechai, and Esther appointed Mordechai over Haman's estate.

[3] Esther then spoke again before the king and fell before his feet. She wept and entreated him to abolish the evil [decree] of Haman the Agagi, and his plan that he had devised against the Jews. [4] The king stretched out the golden scepter

wishes to honor!'" [10] The king then said to Haman, "Quickly take the robes and the horse, as you said, and do this to Mordechai the Jew who sits at the king's [palace] gate. Do not omit anything of whatever you said!" [11] Haman took the robes and the horse and dressed Mordechai [in the robes]. He then rode him in the [main] city square and called out before him, "This is what is done to the man whom the king wishes to honor!" [12] Mordechai then returned to the king's [palace] gate, while Haman hurried to his house, in mourning and his head covered [in dirt]. [13] Haman then told Zeresh, his wife, and all his friends everything that had happened to him. His wise men and Zeresh, his wife, said to him, "If Mordechai, before whom you have begun to fall, is a descendant of the Jews, you will not be able [to harm] him, for you will surely fall before him." [14] They were still speaking with him when the king's attendants arrived, and they rushed to bring Haman to the feast that Esther had prepared.

Chapter 7

[1] The king and Haman then came to drink with Queen Esther. [2] On the second day, as well, at the wine feast, the king asked Esther, "Queen Esther, what is your request and it will be granted you? And what is your wish? [You may ask for] even half the kingdom and [your wish] will be fulfilled." [3] Queen Esther responded and said, "If you regard me favorably, O king, and if it pleases the king, as my request let my life be granted, and as my wish, my people. [4] For I and my people have been sold to be destroyed, killed and annihilated. And if we were sold as slaves and maidservants I would have kept silent, but the oppressor is not concerned about the damage [caused to] the king."

אֲשֶׁר הַמֶּלֶךְ חָפֵץ בִּיקָרוֹ: וַיֹּאמֶר הַמֶּלֶךְ לְהָמָן מַהֵר קַח אֶת־הַלְּבוּשׁ וְאֶת־הַסּוּס כַּאֲשֶׁר דִּבַּרְתָּ וַעֲשֵׂה־כֵן לְמָרְדֳּכַי הַיְּהוּדִי הַיּוֹשֵׁב בְּשַׁעַר הַמֶּלֶךְ אַל־תַּפֵּל דָּבָר מִכֹּל אֲשֶׁר דִּבַּרְתָּ: יא וַיִּקַּח הָמָן אֶת־הַלְּבוּשׁ וְאֶת־הַסּוּס וַיַּלְבֵּשׁ אֶת־מָרְדֳּכָי וַיַּרְכִּיבֵהוּ בִּרְחוֹב הָעִיר וַיִּקְרָא לְפָנָיו כָּכָה יֵעָשֶׂה לָאִישׁ אֲשֶׁר הַמֶּלֶךְ חָפֵץ בִּיקָרוֹ: יב וַיָּשָׁב מָרְדֳּכַי אֶל־שַׁעַר הַמֶּלֶךְ וְהָמָן נִדְחַף אֶל־בֵּיתוֹ אָבֵל וַחֲפוּי רֹאשׁ: יג וַיְסַפֵּר הָמָן לְזֶרֶשׁ אִשְׁתּוֹ וּלְכָל־אֹהֲבָיו אֵת כָּל־אֲשֶׁר קָרָהוּ וַיֹּאמְרוּ לוֹ חֲכָמָיו וְזֶרֶשׁ אִשְׁתּוֹ אִם מִזֶּרַע הַיְּהוּדִים מָרְדֳּכַי אֲשֶׁר הַחִלּוֹתָ לִנְפֹּל לְפָנָיו לֹא־תוּכַל לוֹ כִּי־נָפוֹל תִּפּוֹל לְפָנָיו: יד עוֹדָם מְדַבְּרִים עִמּוֹ וְסָרִיסֵי הַמֶּלֶךְ הִגִּיעוּ וַיַּבְהִלוּ לְהָבִיא אֶת־הָמָן אֶל־הַמִּשְׁתֶּה אֲשֶׁר־עָשְׂתָה אֶסְתֵּר:

פרק ז

א וַיָּבֹא הַמֶּלֶךְ וְהָמָן לִשְׁתּוֹת עִם־אֶסְתֵּר הַמַּלְכָּה: ב וַיֹּאמֶר הַמֶּלֶךְ לְאֶסְתֵּר גַּם בַּיּוֹם הַשֵּׁנִי בְּמִשְׁתֵּה הַיַּיִן מַה־שְּׁאֵלָתֵךְ אֶסְתֵּר הַמַּלְכָּה וְתִנָּתֵן לָךְ וּמַה־בַּקָּשָׁתֵךְ עַד־חֲצִי הַמַּלְכוּת וְתֵעָשׂ: ג וַתַּעַן אֶסְתֵּר הַמַּלְכָּה וַתֹּאמַר אִם־מָצָאתִי חֵן בְּעֵינֶיךָ הַמֶּלֶךְ וְאִם־עַל־הַמֶּלֶךְ טוֹב תִּנָּתֶן־לִי נַפְשִׁי בִּשְׁאֵלָתִי וְעַמִּי בְּבַקָּשָׁתִי: ד כִּי נִמְכַּרְנוּ אֲנִי וְעַמִּי לְהַשְׁמִיד לַהֲרוֹג וּלְאַבֵּד וְאִלּוּ לַעֲבָדִים וְלִשְׁפָחוֹת נִמְכַּרְנוּ הֶחֱרַשְׁתִּי כִּי אֵין הַצָּר שֹׁוֶה בְּנֵזֶק הַמֶּלֶךְ:

מָרְדֳּכַי הַיְּהוּדִי יוֹשֵׁב בְּשַׁעַר הַמֶּלֶךְ: יד וַתֹּאמֶר
לוֹ זֶרֶשׁ אִשְׁתּוֹ וְכָל־אֹהֲבָיו יַעֲשׂוּ־עֵץ גָּבֹהַּ
חֲמִשִּׁים אַמָּה וּבַבֹּקֶר | אֱמֹר לַמֶּלֶךְ וְיִתְלוּ
אֶת־מָרְדֳּכַי עָלָיו וּבֹא עִם־הַמֶּלֶךְ אֶל־הַמִּשְׁתֶּה
שָׂמֵחַ וַיִּיטַב הַדָּבָר לִפְנֵי הָמָן וַיַּעַשׂ הָעֵץ:

פרק ו

א בַּלַּיְלָה הַהוּא נָדְדָה שְׁנַת הַמֶּלֶךְ וַיֹּאמֶר
לְהָבִיא אֶת־סֵפֶר הַזִּכְרֹנוֹת דִּבְרֵי הַיָּמִים וַיִּהְיוּ
נִקְרָאִים לִפְנֵי הַמֶּלֶךְ: ב וַיִּמָּצֵא כָתוּב אֲשֶׁר
הִגִּיד מָרְדֳּכַי עַל־בִּגְתָנָא וָתֶרֶשׁ שְׁנֵי סָרִיסֵי
הַמֶּלֶךְ מִשֹּׁמְרֵי הַסַּף אֲשֶׁר בִּקְשׁוּ לִשְׁלֹחַ יָד
בַּמֶּלֶךְ אֲחַשְׁוֵרוֹשׁ: ג וַיֹּאמֶר הַמֶּלֶךְ מַה־נַּעֲשָׂה
יְקָר וּגְדוּלָּה לְמָרְדֳּכַי עַל־זֶה וַיֹּאמְרוּ נַעֲרֵי
הַמֶּלֶךְ מְשָׁרְתָיו לֹא־נַעֲשָׂה עִמּוֹ דָּבָר: ד וַיֹּאמֶר
הַמֶּלֶךְ מִי בֶחָצֵר וְהָמָן בָּא לַחֲצַר בֵּית־
הַמֶּלֶךְ הַחִיצוֹנָה לֵאמֹר לַמֶּלֶךְ לִתְלוֹת אֶת־
מָרְדֳּכַי עַל־הָעֵץ אֲשֶׁר־הֵכִין לוֹ: ה וַיֹּאמְרוּ נַעֲרֵי
הַמֶּלֶךְ אֵלָיו הִנֵּה הָמָן עֹמֵד בֶּחָצֵר וַיֹּאמֶר
הַמֶּלֶךְ יָבוֹא: ו וַיָּבוֹא הָמָן וַיֹּאמֶר לוֹ הַמֶּלֶךְ
מַה־לַּעֲשׂוֹת בָּאִישׁ אֲשֶׁר הַמֶּלֶךְ חָפֵץ בִּיקָרוֹ
וַיֹּאמֶר הָמָן בְּלִבּוֹ לְמִי יַחְפֹּץ הַמֶּלֶךְ לַעֲשׂוֹת
יְקָר יוֹתֵר מִמֶּנִּי: ז וַיֹּאמֶר הָמָן אֶל־הַמֶּלֶךְ
אִישׁ אֲשֶׁר הַמֶּלֶךְ חָפֵץ בִּיקָרוֹ: ח יָבִיאוּ לְבוּשׁ
מַלְכוּת אֲשֶׁר לָבַשׁ־בּוֹ הַמֶּלֶךְ וְסוּס אֲשֶׁר רָכַב
עָלָיו הַמֶּלֶךְ וַאֲשֶׁר נִתַּן כֶּתֶר מַלְכוּת בְּרֹאשׁוֹ:
ט וְנָתוֹן הַלְּבוּשׁ וְהַסּוּס עַל־יַד־אִישׁ מִשָּׂרֵי
הַמֶּלֶךְ הַפַּרְתְּמִים וְהִלְבִּישׁוּ אֶת־הָאִישׁ אֲשֶׁר
הַמֶּלֶךְ חָפֵץ בִּיקָרוֹ וְהִרְכִּיבֻהוּ עַל־הַסּוּס
בִּרְחוֹב הָעִיר וְקָרְאוּ לְפָנָיו כָּכָה יֵעָשֶׂה לָאִישׁ

workers] make a gallows fifty cubits high, and in the morning tell the king [about it], and they shall hang Mordechai on it; and [then] go with the king to the feast feeling happy!" The idea pleased Haman and he made the gallows.

Chapter 6

That night, sleep eluded the king, so he asked to have the book of records, the chronicles, brought [before him], and they were read out before the king. [2] [There] it was found written that Mordechai had told about Bigsana and Teresh, two of the king's attendants, of the guards of the inner court, who had conspired to act against King Achashverosh. [3] The king then asked, "What honor or [mark of] greatness was [given] to Mordechai for this?" The king's young men, his servants, answered, "Nothing was done for him." [4] The king then asked, "Who is in the courtyard?" and [just then] Haman had come to the outer palace courtyard, to tell the king [his wish] to hang Mordechai on the gallows that he had prepared for him. [5] The king's young men answered [the king], "It is Haman standing in the courtyard." The king said, "Let him enter!" [6] Haman entered, and the king asked him, "What should be done for the man whom the king wishes to honor?" Haman thought to himself, "Who would the king wish to honor more than me?!" [7] So Haman said to the king, "A man whom the king wishes to honor — [8] let [the king's servants] bring the royal robes which the king wore, and the horse on which the king rode [at his coronation], and the royal crown that was [then] placed on his head. [9] Let the robes and the horse then be given under the supervision of one of the king's ministers, [one] of the governors; and [the king's servants] shall dress the man whom the king wishes to honor [in the royal robes], and ride him on the horse in the [main] city square. They shall call out before him, 'This is what is done to the man whom the king

בׁ וַיְהִי כִרְאוֹת הַמֶּלֶךְ אֶת־אֶסְתֵּר הַמַּלְכָּה
עֹמֶדֶת בֶּחָצֵר נָשְׂאָה חֵן בְּעֵינָיו וַיּוֹשֶׁט
הַמֶּלֶךְ לְאֶסְתֵּר אֶת־שַׁרְבִיט הַזָּהָב אֲשֶׁר
בְּיָדוֹ וַתִּקְרַב אֶסְתֵּר וַתִּגַּע בְּרֹאשׁ הַשַּׁרְבִיט:
גׁ וַיֹּאמֶר לָהּ הַמֶּלֶךְ מַה־לָּךְ אֶסְתֵּר הַמַּלְכָּה
וּמַה־בַּקָּשָׁתֵךְ עַד־חֲצִי הַמַּלְכוּת וְיִנָּתֵן לָךְ:
דׁ וַתֹּאמֶר אֶסְתֵּר אִם־עַל־הַמֶּלֶךְ טוֹב יָבוֹא
הַמֶּלֶךְ וְהָמָן הַיּוֹם אֶל־הַמִּשְׁתֶּה אֲשֶׁר־
עָשִׂיתִי לוֹ: הׁ וַיֹּאמֶר הַמֶּלֶךְ מַהֲרוּ אֶת־הָמָן
לַעֲשׂוֹת אֶת־דְּבַר אֶסְתֵּר וַיָּבֹא הַמֶּלֶךְ וְהָמָן
אֶל־הַמִּשְׁתֶּה אֲשֶׁר־עָשְׂתָה אֶסְתֵּר: וׁ וַיֹּאמֶר
הַמֶּלֶךְ לְאֶסְתֵּר בְּמִשְׁתֵּה הַיַּיִן מַה־שְּׁאֵלָתֵךְ
וְיִנָּתֵן לָךְ וּמַה־בַּקָּשָׁתֵךְ עַד־חֲצִי הַמַּלְכוּת
וְתֵעָשׂ: זׁ וַתַּעַן אֶסְתֵּר וַתֹּאמַר שְׁאֵלָתִי
וּבַקָּשָׁתִי: חׁ אִם־מָצָאתִי חֵן בְּעֵינֵי הַמֶּלֶךְ וְאִם־
עַל־הַמֶּלֶךְ טוֹב לָתֵת אֶת־שְׁאֵלָתִי וְלַעֲשׂוֹת
אֶת־בַּקָּשָׁתִי יָבוֹא הַמֶּלֶךְ וְהָמָן אֶל־הַמִּשְׁתֶּה
אֲשֶׁר אֶעֱשֶׂה לָהֶם וּמָחָר אֶעֱשֶׂה כִּדְבַר
הַמֶּלֶךְ: טׁ וַיֵּצֵא הָמָן בַּיּוֹם הַהוּא שָׂמֵחַ וְטוֹב
לֵב וְכִרְאוֹת הָמָן אֶת־מָרְדֳּכַי בְּשַׁעַר הַמֶּלֶךְ
וְלֹא־קָם וְלֹא־זָע מִמֶּנּוּ וַיִּמָּלֵא הָמָן עַל־מָרְדֳּכַי
חֵמָה: יׁ וַיִּתְאַפַּק הָמָן וַיָּבוֹא אֶל־בֵּיתוֹ וַיִּשְׁלַח
וַיָּבֵא אֶת־אֹהֲבָיו וְאֶת־זֶרֶשׁ אִשְׁתּוֹ: יאׁ וַיְסַפֵּר
לָהֶם הָמָן אֶת־כְּבוֹד עָשְׁרוֹ וְרֹב בָּנָיו וְאֵת
כָּל־אֲשֶׁר גִּדְּלוֹ הַמֶּלֶךְ וְאֵת אֲשֶׁר נִשְּׂאוֹ עַל־
הַשָּׂרִים וְעַבְדֵי הַמֶּלֶךְ: יבׁ וַיֹּאמֶר הָמָן אַף
לֹא־הֵבִיאָה אֶסְתֵּר הַמַּלְכָּה עִם־הַמֶּלֶךְ אֶל־
הַמִּשְׁתֶּה אֲשֶׁר־עָשָׂתָה כִּי אִם־אוֹתִי וְגַם־
לְמָחָר אֲנִי קָרוּא־לָהּ עִם־הַמֶּלֶךְ: יגׁ וְכָל־זֶה
אֵינֶנּוּ שֹׁוֶה לִי בְּכָל־עֵת אֲשֶׁר אֲנִי רֹאֶה אֶת־

of the chamber. ² Then, when the king saw Queen Esther standing in the courtyard, she found favor in his eyes, and the king stretched out the golden scepter in his hand to Esther. Esther then approached and touched the tip of the scepter. ³The king then said to her, "Queen Esther, what do you want and what is your wish? [You may ask for] even half the kingdom and it will be granted you." ⁴ Esther replied, "If it pleases the king, may the king, with Haman, come today to the feast that I have prepared for him." ⁵ The king then said, "Quickly bring Haman to carry out what Esther has said," and [so] the king and Haman came to the feast that Esther had prepared. ⁶ The king said to Esther at the wine feast, "What is your request and it will be granted you? And what is your wish? [You may ask for] even half the kingdom and [your wish] will be fulfilled." ⁷ Esther responded and said, "[This is] my request and my wish. ⁸ If the king regards me favorably, and if it pleases the king to fulfill my request and to carry out my wish, may the king, with Haman, come to the feast that I shall prepare for them, and tomorrow I shall carry out what the king has [asked]." ⁹ Haman left [the king] on that day happy and in good spirits, but when Haman saw Mordechai at the king's [palace] gate, and he did not rise or [even] move [out of respect] for him, Haman was filled with rage against Mordechai. ¹⁰ Haman restrained himself and came to his house. He then sent for and brought [together] his friends and Zeresh, his wife. ¹¹ Haman told them about the honor [he received from] his wealth, and about his great number of children, and how the king had promoted him and raised his position over the ministers and the king's servants. ¹² Haman then said, "Even Queen Esther did not bring anyone [else] with the king, except me, to the feast she prepared, and tomorrow, as well, I am invited to her [feast] with the king. ¹³All this, [however,] is worth nothing to me, every time I see Mordechai the Jew sitting at the king's [palace] gate!" ¹⁴ Zeresh his wife, with all his friends, then said to him, "Let [the weighed out for the king's treasuries in [exchange for] the Jews, so as to annihilate them. 8 And he gave him the text of the document of law that was issued in Shushan to destroy [the Jews], to show [it] to Esther and to tell her [what had happened], and to order her to go to the king to entreat him and beseech him on behalf of her people. 9 Hasach went and told Esther, Mordechai's words. 10 Esther then said to Hasach, and instructed him to [tell] Mordechai, 11 "All the king's servants and the people of the king's states know, that any man or woman who comes to the king, to the inner courtyard, without being called, there is one law for him: to be put to death; only he to whom the king stretches out the golden scepter will live. I, [however,] have not been called to come to the king for the past thirty days." 12 They then told Mordechai what Esther had said. 13 Mordechai then told [them] to convey to Esther, "Do not imagine [you can] save yourself in the king's palace from [the fate of] all the Jews. 14 For if you indeed keep silent at this time, relief and salvation will come to the Jews from another source, and you and your father's household will perish. And who knows if in a year's time you will hold the same royal position?!" 15 Esther then told [them] to convey to Mordechai, 16 "Go [and] gather all the Jews located in Shushan, and [proclaim a] fast on my behalf, that you will not eat and drink for three days, night and day. I, with my maids, will also fast in this way. And thus I will go to the king, [though] it is against the law, and if I perish, I perish." 17 Mordechai [thus] crossed over and did according to everything that Esther instructed him.

Chapter 5

Then, on the third day, Esther put on [her] royal [robes] and stood in the inner courtyard of the king's palace, directly facing the king's chamber, while the king was sitting on his royal throne in the royal chamber, facing the entrance

אֶסְתֵּר וּלְהַגִּיד לָהּ וּלְצַוּוֹת עָלֶיהָ לָבוֹא אֶל־הַמֶּלֶךְ לְהִתְחַנֶּן־לוֹ וּלְבַקֵּשׁ מִלְּפָנָיו עַל־עַמָּהּ: טוַיָּבוֹא הֲתָךְ וַיַּגֵּד לְאֶסְתֵּר אֵת דִּבְרֵי מָרְדֳּכָי: יוַתֹּאמֶר אֶסְתֵּר לַהֲתָךְ וַתְּצַוֵּהוּ אֶל־מָרְדֳּכָי: יאכָּל־עַבְדֵי הַמֶּלֶךְ וְעַם־מְדִינוֹת הַמֶּלֶךְ יֹדְעִים אֲשֶׁר כָּל־אִישׁ וְאִשָּׁה אֲשֶׁר־יָבוֹא אֶל־הַמֶּלֶךְ אֶל־הֶחָצֵר הַפְּנִימִית אֲשֶׁר לֹא־יִקָּרֵא אַחַת דָּתוֹ לְהָמִית לְבַד מֵאֲשֶׁר יוֹשִׁיט־לוֹ הַמֶּלֶךְ אֶת־שַׁרְבִיט הַזָּהָב וְחָיָה וַאֲנִי לֹא נִקְרֵאתִי לָבוֹא אֶל־הַמֶּלֶךְ זֶה שְׁלוֹשִׁים יוֹם: יבוַיַּגִּידוּ לְמָרְדֳּכָי אֵת דִּבְרֵי אֶסְתֵּר: יגוַיֹּאמֶר מָרְדֳּכַי לְהָשִׁיב אֶל־אֶסְתֵּר אַל־תְּדַמִּי בְנַפְשֵׁךְ לְהִמָּלֵט בֵּית־הַמֶּלֶךְ מִכָּל־הַיְּהוּדִים: ידכִּי אִם־הַחֲרֵשׁ תַּחֲרִישִׁי בָּעֵת הַזֹּאת רֶוַח וְהַצָּלָה יַעֲמוֹד לַיְּהוּדִים מִמָּקוֹם אַחֵר וְאַתְּ וּבֵית־אָבִיךְ תֹּאבֵדוּ וּמִי יוֹדֵעַ אִם־לְעֵת כָּזֹאת הִגַּעַתְּ לַמַּלְכוּת: טווַתֹּאמֶר אֶסְתֵּר לְהָשִׁיב אֶל־מָרְדֳּכָי: טזלֵךְ כְּנוֹס אֶת־כָּל־הַיְּהוּדִים הַנִּמְצְאִים בְּשׁוּשָׁן וְצוּמוּ עָלַי וְאַל־תֹּאכְלוּ וְאַל־תִּשְׁתּוּ שְׁלֹשֶׁת יָמִים לַיְלָה וָיוֹם גַּם־אֲנִי וְנַעֲרֹתַי אָצוּם כֵּן וּבְכֵן אָבוֹא אֶל־הַמֶּלֶךְ אֲשֶׁר לֹא־כַדָּת וְכַאֲשֶׁר אָבַדְתִּי אָבָדְתִּי: יזוַיַּעֲבֹר מָרְדֳּכָי וַיַּעַשׂ כְּכֹל אֲשֶׁר־צִוְּתָה עָלָיו אֶסְתֵּר:

פרק ה

אוַיְהִי | בַּיּוֹם הַשְּׁלִישִׁי וַתִּלְבַּשׁ אֶסְתֵּר מַלְכוּת וַתַּעֲמֹד בַּחֲצַר בֵּית־הַמֶּלֶךְ הַפְּנִימִית נֹכַח בֵּית הַמֶּלֶךְ וְהַמֶּלֶךְ יוֹשֵׁב עַל־כִּסֵּא מַלְכוּתוֹ בְּבֵית הַמַּלְכוּת נֹכַח פֶּתַח הַבָּיִת:

עֲשָׂר הוּא־חֹדֶשׁ אֲדָר וּשְׁלָלָם לָבוֹז: יד פַּתְשֶׁגֶן הַכְּתָב לְהִנָּתֵן דָּת בְּכָל־מְדִינָה וּמְדִינָה גָּלוּי לְכָל־הָעַמִּים לִהְיוֹת עֲתִדִים לַיּוֹם הַזֶּה: טו הָרָצִים יָצְאוּ דְחוּפִים בִּדְבַר הַמֶּלֶךְ וְהַדָּת נִתְּנָה בְּשׁוּשַׁן הַבִּירָה וְהַמֶּלֶךְ וְהָמָן יָשְׁבוּ לִשְׁתּוֹת וְהָעִיר שׁוּשָׁן נָבוֹכָה:

פרק ד

א וּמָרְדֳּכַי יָדַע אֶת־כָּל־אֲשֶׁר נַעֲשָׂה וַיִּקְרַע מָרְדֳּכַי אֶת־בְּגָדָיו וַיִּלְבַּשׁ שַׂק וָאֵפֶר וַיֵּצֵא בְּתוֹךְ הָעִיר וַיִּזְעַק זְעָקָה גְדוֹלָה וּמָרָה: ב וַיָּבוֹא עַד לִפְנֵי שַׁעַר־הַמֶּלֶךְ כִּי אֵין לָבוֹא אֶל־שַׁעַר הַמֶּלֶךְ בִּלְבוּשׁ שָׂק: ג וּבְכָל־ מְדִינָה וּמְדִינָה מְקוֹם אֲשֶׁר דְּבַר־הַמֶּלֶךְ וְדָתוֹ מַגִּיעַ אֵבֶל גָּדוֹל לַיְּהוּדִים וְצוֹם וּבְכִי וּמִסְפֵּד שַׂק וָאֵפֶר יֻצַּע לָרַבִּים: ד וְתָבוֹאינָה כתיב וַתָּבוֹאנָה נַעֲרוֹת אֶסְתֵּר וְסָרִיסֶיהָ וַיַּגִּידוּ לָהּ וַתִּתְחַלְחַל הַמַּלְכָּה מְאֹד וַתִּשְׁלַח בְּגָדִים לְהַלְבִּישׁ אֶת־מָרְדֳּכַי וּלְהָסִיר שַׂקּוֹ מֵעָלָיו וְלֹא קִבֵּל: ה וַתִּקְרָא אֶסְתֵּר לַהֲתָךְ מִסָּרִיסֵי הַמֶּלֶךְ אֲשֶׁר הֶעֱמִיד לְפָנֶיהָ וַתְּצַוֵּהוּ עַל־ מָרְדֳּכָי לָדַעַת מַה־זֶּה וְעַל־מַה־זֶּה: ו וַיֵּצֵא הֲתָךְ אֶל־מָרְדֳּכָי אֶל־רְחוֹב הָעִיר אֲשֶׁר לִפְנֵי שַׁעַר־הַמֶּלֶךְ: ז וַיַּגֶּד־לוֹ מָרְדֳּכַי אֵת כָּל־אֲשֶׁר קָרָהוּ וְאֵת | פָּרָשַׁת הַכֶּסֶף אֲשֶׁר אָמַר הָמָן לִשְׁקוֹל עַל־גִּנְזֵי הַמֶּלֶךְ ביהודיים כתיב בַּיְּהוּדִים לְאַבְּדָם: ח וְאֶת־פַּתְשֶׁגֶן כְּתָב־הַדָּת אֲשֶׁר נִתַּן בְּשׁוּשָׁן לְהַשְׁמִידָם נָתַן לוֹ לְהַרְאוֹת אֶת־

sent by runners to all the king's states, [ordering them] to destroy, kill and annihilate all the Jews, both young and old, children and women, on one day — the thirteenth of the twelfth month, the month of Adar — and to plunder their [property as] spoil. [14] The text of the document was to become law in every state [and] publicized to all the peoples, for [them] to be prepared for this day. [15] The runners set out in haste with the king's decree and the law was published in the citadel of Shushan. The king and Haman then sat down to drink, while [the Jews of] the city of Shushan [were] bewildered.

Chapter 4

Mordechai, [however,] was aware of everything that had happened, so Mordechai tore his clothes and put on sackcloth and ashes. He then went out in the center of the city and let out a great and bitter cry. [2] He came [only] as far as the front of the king's [palace] gate, for one did not enter the king's [palace] gate with sackcloth clothing. [3] And in every state, wherever the king's decree reached and his law [took effect], there was great mourning for the Jews, with fasting, weeping and lamenting; sackcloth and ashes were worn by many. [4] Esther's maids and attendants came and told her [about Mordechai,] and the queen was extremely shocked. She sent clothes to dress Mordechai [properly so that he may] remove his sackcloth, but he did not accept [them]. [5] Esther then summoned Hasach, [one] of the king's attendants whom he appointed to be before her, and she instructed him about Mordechai, to find out [for] what was this [weeping], and why [he did not accept the clothes]. [6] Hasach went out to Mordechai, to the [main] city square which was in front of the king's [palace] gate. [7] Mordechai told him everything that had happened to him, and [about] the setting aside of the money — that Haman had said [he would have the money]

בְּמָרְדֳּכַי לְבַדּוֹ כִּי־הִגִּידוּ לוֹ אֶת־עַם מָרְדֳּכָי
וַיְבַקֵּשׁ הָמָן לְהַשְׁמִיד אֶת־כָּל־הַיְּהוּדִים
אֲשֶׁר בְּכָל־מַלְכוּת אֲחַשְׁוֵרוֹשׁ עַם מָרְדֳּכָי:
בַּחֹדֶשׁ הָרִאשׁוֹן הוּא־חֹדֶשׁ נִיסָן בִּשְׁנַת
שְׁתֵּים עֶשְׂרֵה לַמֶּלֶךְ אֲחַשְׁוֵרוֹשׁ הִפִּיל פּוּר
הוּא הַגּוֹרָל לִפְנֵי הָמָן מִיּוֹם | לְיוֹם וּמֵחֹדֶשׁ
לְחֹדֶשׁ שְׁנֵים־עָשָׂר הוּא־חֹדֶשׁ אֲדָר:

ח וַיֹּאמֶר הָמָן לַמֶּלֶךְ אֲחַשְׁוֵרוֹשׁ יֶשְׁנוֹ עַם־
אֶחָד מְפֻזָּר וּמְפֹרָד בֵּין הָעַמִּים בְּכֹל מְדִינוֹת
מַלְכוּתֶךָ וְדָתֵיהֶם שֹׁנוֹת מִכָּל־עָם וְאֶת־
דָּתֵי הַמֶּלֶךְ אֵינָם עֹשִׂים וְלַמֶּלֶךְ אֵין־שֹׁוֶה
לְהַנִּיחָם: ט אִם־עַל־הַמֶּלֶךְ טוֹב יִכָּתֵב לְאַבְּדָם
וַעֲשֶׂרֶת אֲלָפִים כִּכַּר־כֶּסֶף אֶשְׁקוֹל עַל־
יְדֵי עֹשֵׂי הַמְּלָאכָה לְהָבִיא אֶל־גִּנְזֵי הַמֶּלֶךְ:
י וַיָּסַר הַמֶּלֶךְ אֶת־טַבַּעְתּוֹ מֵעַל יָדוֹ וַיִּתְּנָהּ
לְהָמָן בֶּן־הַמְּדָתָא הָאֲגָגִי צֹרֵר הַיְּהוּדִים:
יא וַיֹּאמֶר הַמֶּלֶךְ לְהָמָן הַכֶּסֶף נָתוּן לָךְ
וְהָעָם לַעֲשׂוֹת בּוֹ כַּטּוֹב בְּעֵינֶיךָ: יב וַיִּקָּרְאוּ
סֹפְרֵי הַמֶּלֶךְ בַּחֹדֶשׁ הָרִאשׁוֹן בִּשְׁלוֹשָׁה
עָשָׂר יוֹם בּוֹ וַיִּכָּתֵב כְּכָל־אֲשֶׁר־צִוָּה הָמָן אֶל
אֲחַשְׁדַּרְפְּנֵי־הַמֶּלֶךְ וְאֶל־הַפַּחוֹת אֲשֶׁר | עַל־
מְדִינָה וּמְדִינָה וְאֶל־שָׂרֵי עַם וָעָם מְדִינָה
וּמְדִינָה כִּכְתָבָהּ וְעַם וָעָם כִּלְשֹׁנוֹ בְּשֵׁם
הַמֶּלֶךְ אֲחַשְׁוֵרֹשׁ נִכְתָּב וְנֶחְתָּם בְּטַבַּעַת
הַמֶּלֶךְ: יג וְנִשְׁלוֹחַ סְפָרִים בְּיַד הָרָצִים אֶל־
כָּל־מְדִינוֹת הַמֶּלֶךְ לְהַשְׁמִיד לַהֲרֹג וּלְאַבֵּד
אֶת־כָּל־הַיְּהוּדִים מִנַּעַר וְעַד־זָקֵן טַף וְנָשִׁים
בְּיוֹם אֶחָד בִּשְׁלוֹשָׁה עָשָׂר לְחֹדֶשׁ שְׁנֵים־

him day after day but he did not listen to them, they told Haman [about it], to see if Mordechai's words would hold firm, for he had told them that [he did not bow down because] he was a Jew. [5] Haman then saw that Mordechai was not bowing down or prostrating himself to him and Haman was filled with rage. [6] He regarded it below his dignity, [though,] to act against Mordechai alone, [and] since they had told him to which people Mordechai belonged, Haman wished to destroy all the Jews who were in the entire kingdom of Achashverosh — Mordechai's people. [7] In the first month, the month of Nisan, in the twelfth year of King Achashverosh, [someone] cast *pur*, which is the lot, before Haman, [to select] which day and which month, [and it came out] to the twelfth month, the month of Adar.

[8] Haman then said to King Achashverosh, "There is a certain people, scattered and spread out among the [other] peoples in all the states of your kingdom, and their laws are different from [those of] other peoples and they do not observe the king's laws, so it is not worth it for the king to leave them alive. [9] If it pleases the king, let [a decree] be written to annihilate them, and I shall have ten thousand talents of silver weighed out by the mint to be brought to the king's treasuries." [10] The king then removed his signet ring from his hand and gave it to Haman the son of Hamedasa, the Agagi, the oppressor of the Jews. [11] The king said to Haman, "The silver is given to you [to keep], and the people, [as well,] to do with them as you please." [12] The king's scribes were then summoned in the first month, on the thirteenth day of [the month], and whatever Haman commanded the king's satraps and governors who [ruled] over each state, and the ministers of each people, was written down; [to] each state according to its [form of] script, and [to] each people according to its language. It was written in the name of King Achashverosh and sealed with the king's signet ring. [13] Bills [of law] were to be

הַמֶּלֶךְ מִשְׁתֶּה גָדוֹל לְכָל־שָׂרָיו וַעֲבָדָיו אֵת
מִשְׁתֵּה אֶסְתֵּר וַהֲנָחָה לַמְּדִינוֹת עָשָׂה וַיִּתֵּן
מַשְׂאֵת כְּיַד הַמֶּלֶךְ: יט וּבְהִקָּבֵץ בְּתוּלוֹת
שֵׁנִית וּמָרְדֳּכַי יֹשֵׁב בְּשַׁעַר־הַמֶּלֶךְ: כ אֵין
אֶסְתֵּר מַגֶּדֶת מוֹלַדְתָּהּ וְאֶת־עַמָּהּ כַּאֲשֶׁר
צִוָּה עָלֶיהָ מָרְדֳּכָי וְאֶת־מַאֲמַר מָרְדֳּכַי אֶסְתֵּר
עֹשָׂה כַּאֲשֶׁר הָיְתָה בְאָמְנָה אִתּוֹ:

כא בַּיָּמִים הָהֵם וּמָרְדֳּכַי יוֹשֵׁב בְּשַׁעַר־הַמֶּלֶךְ
קָצַף בִּגְתָן וָתֶרֶשׁ שְׁנֵי־סָרִיסֵי הַמֶּלֶךְ מִשֹּׁמְרֵי
הַסַּף וַיְבַקְשׁוּ לִשְׁלֹחַ יָד בַּמֶּלֶךְ אֲחַשְׁוֵרֹשׁ:
כב וַיִּוָּדַע הַדָּבָר לְמָרְדֳּכַי וַיַּגֵּד לְאֶסְתֵּר
הַמַּלְכָּה וַתֹּאמֶר אֶסְתֵּר לַמֶּלֶךְ בְּשֵׁם מָרְדֳּכָי:
כג וַיְבֻקַּשׁ הַדָּבָר וַיִּמָּצֵא וַיִּתָּלוּ שְׁנֵיהֶם עַל־עֵץ
וַיִּכָּתֵב בְּסֵפֶר דִּבְרֵי הַיָּמִים לִפְנֵי הַמֶּלֶךְ:

פרק ג

א אַחַר | הַדְּבָרִים הָאֵלֶּה גִּדַּל הַמֶּלֶךְ
אֲחַשְׁוֵרוֹשׁ אֶת־הָמָן בֶּן־הַמְּדָתָא הָאֲגָגִי
וַיְנַשְּׂאֵהוּ וַיָּשֶׂם אֶת־כִּסְאוֹ מֵעַל כָּל־הַשָּׂרִים
אֲשֶׁר אִתּוֹ: ב וְכָל־עַבְדֵי הַמֶּלֶךְ אֲשֶׁר־בְּשַׁעַר
הַמֶּלֶךְ כֹּרְעִים וּמִשְׁתַּחֲוִים לְהָמָן כִּי־כֵן צִוָּה־
לוֹ הַמֶּלֶךְ וּמָרְדֳּכַי לֹא יִכְרַע וְלֹא יִשְׁתַּחֲוֶה:
ג וַיֹּאמְרוּ עַבְדֵי הַמֶּלֶךְ אֲשֶׁר־בְּשַׁעַר הַמֶּלֶךְ
לְמָרְדֳּכָי מַדּוּעַ אַתָּה עוֹבֵר אֵת מִצְוַת הַמֶּלֶךְ:
ד וַיְהִי באמרם כתיב כְּאָמְרָם אֵלָיו יוֹם וָיוֹם וְלֹא
שָׁמַע אֲלֵיהֶם וַיַּגִּידוּ לְהָמָן לִרְאוֹת הֲיַעַמְדוּ
דִּבְרֵי מָרְדֳּכַי כִּי־הִגִּיד לָהֶם אֲשֶׁר־הוּא יְהוּדִי:
ה וַיַּרְא הָמָן כִּי־אֵין מָרְדֳּכַי כֹּרֵעַ וּמִשְׁתַּחֲוֶה
לוֹ וַיִּמָּלֵא הָמָן חֵמָה: ו וַיִּבֶז בְּעֵינָיו לִשְׁלֹחַ יָד

favor before him more than all the [other] maidens, so he placed the royal crown on her head, and made her queen in place of Vashti. [18] The king then made a great banquet for all his ministers and servants, [calling it] Esther's banquet, and made a [tax] concession for the states and gave [them] king-size gifts. [19] And when the maidens were brought together a second time, [nevertheless, since] Mordechai was sitting at the king's [palace] gate, [20] Esther would not tell [the king] her lineage or nationality, just as Mordechai had ordered her. Esther [also] carried out all [the laws] that Mordechai had told her [to do], just as when she was in his care.

[21] At that time, when Mordechai was sitting at the king's [palace] gate, Bigsan and Teresh, two attendants of the king, of the guards of the inner court, were angry, and conspired to act against King Achashverosh. [22] Mordechai found out about the [conspiracy] and told Queen Esther [about it]. Esther then informed the king, in the name of Mordechai. [23] The matter was then investigated and found [to be true], and both [Bigsan and Teresh] were hanged on a gallows. [Mordechai's deed] was written down in the book of chronicles [that was kept] before the king.

Chapter 3

After these events, King Achashverosh promoted Haman the son of Hamedasa, the Agagi, and raised his status, and made his position higher than all the [other] ministers who were with him. [2] And all the king's servants who were at the king's [palace] gate were bowing down and prostrating themselves to Haman, for so the king had commanded regarding him, but Mordechai would not bow down or prostrate himself. [3] The king's servants who were at the king's [palace] gate then said to Mordechai, "Why do you disobey the king's command?" [4] When they said [this] to

הַנָּשִׁים: ט וַתִּיטַב הַנַּעֲרָה בְעֵינָיו וַתִּשָּׂא חֶסֶד לְפָנָיו וַיְבַהֵל אֶת־תַּמְרוּקֶיהָ וְאֶת־מָנוֹתֶהָ לָתֵת לָהּ וְאֵת שֶׁבַע הַנְּעָרוֹת הָרְאֻיוֹת לָתֶת־לָהּ מִבֵּית הַמֶּלֶךְ וַיְשַׁנֶּהָ וְאֶת־נַעֲרוֹתֶיהָ לְטוֹב בֵּית הַנָּשִׁים: י לֹא־הִגִּידָה אֶסְתֵּר אֶת־עַמָּהּ וְאֶת־מוֹלַדְתָּהּ כִּי מָרְדֳּכַי צִוָּה עָלֶיהָ אֲשֶׁר לֹא־תַגִּיד: יא וּבְכָל־יוֹם וָיוֹם מָרְדֳּכַי מִתְהַלֵּךְ לִפְנֵי חֲצַר בֵּית־הַנָּשִׁים לָדַעַת אֶת־שְׁלוֹם אֶסְתֵּר וּמַה־יֵּעָשֶׂה בָּהּ: יב וּבְהַגִּיעַ תֹּר נַעֲרָה וְנַעֲרָה לָבוֹא | אֶל־הַמֶּלֶךְ אֲחַשְׁוֵרוֹשׁ מִקֵּץ הֱיוֹת לָהּ כְּדָת הַנָּשִׁים שְׁנֵים עָשָׂר חֹדֶשׁ כִּי כֵּן יִמְלְאוּ יְמֵי מְרוּקֵיהֶן שִׁשָּׁה חֳדָשִׁים בְּשֶׁמֶן הַמֹּר וְשִׁשָּׁה חֳדָשִׁים בַּבְּשָׂמִים וּבְתַמְרוּקֵי הַנָּשִׁים: יג וּבָזֶה הַנַּעֲרָה בָּאָה אֶל־הַמֶּלֶךְ אֵת כָּל־אֲשֶׁר תֹּאמַר יִנָּתֵן לָהּ לָבוֹא עִמָּהּ מִבֵּית הַנָּשִׁים עַד־בֵּית הַמֶּלֶךְ: יד בָּעֶרֶב | הִיא בָאָה וּבַבֹּקֶר הִיא שָׁבָה אֶל־בֵּית הַנָּשִׁים שֵׁנִי אֶל־ יַד שַׁעֲשְׁגַז סְרִיס הַמֶּלֶךְ שֹׁמֵר הַפִּילַגְשִׁים לֹא־תָבוֹא עוֹד אֶל־הַמֶּלֶךְ כִּי אִם־חָפֵץ בָּהּ הַמֶּלֶךְ וְנִקְרְאָה בְשֵׁם: טו וּבְהַגִּיעַ תֹּר־אֶסְתֵּר בַּת־אֲבִיחַיִל דֹּד מָרְדֳּכַי אֲשֶׁר לָקַח־לוֹ לְבַת לָבוֹא אֶל־הַמֶּלֶךְ לֹא בִקְשָׁה דָּבָר כִּי אִם אֶת־ אֲשֶׁר יֹאמַר הֵגַי סְרִיס־הַמֶּלֶךְ שֹׁמֵר הַנָּשִׁים וַתְּהִי אֶסְתֵּר נֹשֵׂאת חֵן בְּעֵינֵי כָּל־רֹאֶיהָ: טז וַתִּלָּקַח אֶסְתֵּר אֶל־הַמֶּלֶךְ אֲחַשְׁוֵרוֹשׁ אֶל־ בֵּית מַלְכוּתוֹ בַּחֹדֶשׁ הָעֲשִׂירִי הוּא־חֹדֶשׁ טֵבֵת בִּשְׁנַת־שֶׁבַע לְמַלְכוּתוֹ: יז וַיֶּאֱהַב הַמֶּלֶךְ אֶת־אֶסְתֵּר מִכָּל־הַנָּשִׁים וַתִּשָּׂא־חֵן וָחֶסֶד לְפָנָיו מִכָּל־הַבְּתוּלוֹת וַיָּשֶׂם כֶּתֶר־מַלְכוּת בְּרֹאשָׁהּ וַיַּמְלִיכֶהָ תַּחַת וַשְׁתִּי: יח וַיַּעַשׂ

brought together to the citadel of Shushan, into the charge of Hegai, that Esther was [also] taken to the king's palace, into the charge of Hegai, the guardian of the women. [9] The girl was pleasing to him and carried favor with him, so he hurriedly brought her her cosmetics and her portions [of food], and the seven maids she was allocated from the king's palace [to serve her], and he gave her and her maids preferential treatment [at] the women's residence. [10] Esther did not tell [them] her nationality or lineage, because Mordechai had ordered her that she must not tell. [11] And each day Mordechai would walk in front of the courtyard of the women's residence, to find out how Esther was faring and what was happening to her. [12] And when the time came for each girl to go to King Achashverosh — at the end of her having had the prescribed [time] for women, twelve months, for that is the duration of their cosmetic process: six months with myrrh oil and six months with perfumes and women's cosmetics — [13] in this [way] the girl would go to the king: whatever she asked would be given to her, to accompany her from the women's residence to the king's palace. [14] In the evening she would go [to the king], and in the morning she would return to the second women's residence, into the charge of Sha'ashgaz, the king's attendant, the guardian of the concubines. She would not go again to the king, unless the king desired her and she was called by name. [15] And when the time came for Esther — the daughter of Avichayil, the uncle of Mordechai who had taken [her] for himself as a [wife] — to go to the king, she did not request anything, except for what Hegai, the king's attendant, the guardian of the women, would say [be given to her]. [Nevertheless,] Esther carried charm before everyone who saw her. [16] Esther was taken to King Achashverosh, to his royal palace, in the tenth month, which is the month of Teves, in the seventh year of his reign. [17] The king loved Esther more than all the [other] women, and she carried charm and

הַמֶּלֶךְ וְהַשָּׂרִים וַיַּעַשׂ הַמֶּלֶךְ כִּדְבַר מְמוּכָן: כב וַיִּשְׁלַח סְפָרִים אֶל־כָּל־מְדִינוֹת הַמֶּלֶךְ אֶל־מְדִינָה וּמְדִינָה כִּכְתָבָהּ וְאֶל־עַם וָעָם כִּלְשׁוֹנוֹ לִהְיוֹת כָּל־אִישׁ שֹׂרֵר בְּבֵיתוֹ וּמְדַבֵּר כִּלְשׁוֹן עַמּוֹ:

פרק ב

א אַחַר הַדְּבָרִים הָאֵלֶּה כְּשֹׁךְ חֲמַת הַמֶּלֶךְ אֲחַשְׁוֵרוֹשׁ זָכַר אֶת־וַשְׁתִּי וְאֵת אֲשֶׁר־עָשָׂתָה וְאֵת אֲשֶׁר־נִגְזַר עָלֶיהָ: ב וַיֹּאמְרוּ נַעֲרֵי־הַמֶּלֶךְ מְשָׁרְתָיו יְבַקְשׁוּ לַמֶּלֶךְ נְעָרוֹת בְּתוּלוֹת טוֹבוֹת מַרְאֶה: ג וְיַפְקֵד הַמֶּלֶךְ פְּקִידִים בְּכָל־מְדִינוֹת מַלְכוּתוֹ וְיִקְבְּצוּ אֶת־כָּל־נַעֲרָה־בְתוּלָה טוֹבַת מַרְאֶה אֶל־שׁוּשַׁן הַבִּירָה אֶל־בֵּית הַנָּשִׁים אֶל־יַד הֵגֶא סְרִיס הַמֶּלֶךְ שֹׁמֵר הַנָּשִׁים וְנָתוֹן תַּמְרֻקֵיהֶן: ד וְהַנַּעֲרָה אֲשֶׁר תִּיטַב בְּעֵינֵי הַמֶּלֶךְ תִּמְלֹךְ תַּחַת וַשְׁתִּי וַיִּיטַב הַדָּבָר בְּעֵינֵי הַמֶּלֶךְ וַיַּעַשׂ כֵּן:

ה אִישׁ יְהוּדִי הָיָה בְּשׁוּשַׁן הַבִּירָה וּשְׁמוֹ מָרְדֳּכַי בֶּן יָאִיר בֶּן־שִׁמְעִי בֶּן־קִישׁ אִישׁ יְמִינִי: ו אֲשֶׁר הָגְלָה מִירוּשָׁלַיִם עִם־הַגֹּלָה אֲשֶׁר הָגְלְתָה עִם יְכָנְיָה מֶלֶךְ־יְהוּדָה אֲשֶׁר הֶגְלָה נְבוּכַדְנֶצַּר מֶלֶךְ בָּבֶל: ז וַיְהִי אֹמֵן אֶת־הֲדַסָּה הִיא אֶסְתֵּר בַּת־דֹּדוֹ כִּי אֵין לָהּ אָב וָאֵם וְהַנַּעֲרָה יְפַת־תֹּאַר וְטוֹבַת מַרְאֶה וּבְמוֹת אָבִיהָ וְאִמָּהּ לְקָחָהּ מָרְדֳּכַי לוֹ לְבַת: ח וַיְהִי בְּהִשָּׁמַע דְּבַר־הַמֶּלֶךְ וְדָתוֹ וּבְהִקָּבֵץ נְעָרוֹת רַבּוֹת אֶל־שׁוּשַׁן הַבִּירָה אֶל־יַד הֵגָי וַתִּלָּקַח אֶסְתֵּר אֶל־בֵּית הַמֶּלֶךְ אֶל־יַד הֵגַי שֹׁמֵר

for it is a great [decree], and [thus] all women will give respect to their husbands, whether great or insignificant." [21] The matter pleased the king and the ministers, and the king carried out what Memuchan had said. [22] He sent bills [of law] to all the king's states, to each state according to its [form of] script, and to each nation according to its language, [stating] that every man be the ruler in his house, and that [his wife] speak his language.

Chapter 2

After these events, when King Achashverosh's anger had abated, he remembered Vashti and what she had done, and what had been decreed upon her. [2] So the king's young men, his servants, said to him, "Let [the king's messengers] look for good-looking maidens for the king. [3] Let the king appoint officers in all the states of his kingdom, and they shall bring together every good-looking maiden to the citadel of Shushan, to the women's residence, into the charge of Hegey, the king's attendant, the guardian of the women, with their cosmetics being provided. [4] Then, the young girl who is pleasing in the eyes of the king shall become queen instead of Vashti." The idea pleased the king and he did so.

[5] There was a Jewish man in the citadel of Shushan, whose name was Mordechai, the son of Ya'ir, the son of Shim'iy, the son of Kish, a man of [the tribe of] Binyamin; [6] who had been exiled from Jerusalem, with the exile that was exiled with Yechonyah, the king of Judea, whom Nebuchadnezzar, the king of Babylonia, had exiled. [7] He took care of Hadassah — that is Esther, his cousin — for she had no father or mother. Now, the girl was beautifully formed and of fine appearance, and when her father and mother died, Mordechai took her for himself as a daughter. [8] It was then, when the king's proclamation and law were publicized, and many girls were

וְהַשָּׁרִים אֶת־יָפְיָהּ כִּי־טוֹבַת מַרְאֶה הִיא: יבוַתְּמָאֵן הַמַּלְכָּה וַשְׁתִּי לָבוֹא בִּדְבַר הַמֶּלֶךְ אֲשֶׁר בְּיַד הַסָּרִיסִים וַיִּקְצֹף הַמֶּלֶךְ מְאֹד וַחֲמָתוֹ בָּעֲרָה בוֹ:

יגוַיֹּאמֶר הַמֶּלֶךְ לַחֲכָמִים יֹדְעֵי הָעִתִּים כִּי־כֵן דְּבַר הַמֶּלֶךְ לִפְנֵי כָּל־יֹדְעֵי דָּת וָדִין: ידוְהַקָּרֹב אֵלָיו כַּרְשְׁנָא שֵׁתָר אַדְמָתָא תַרְשִׁישׁ מֶרֶס מַרְסְנָא מְמוּכָן שִׁבְעַת שָׂרֵי | פָּרַס וּמָדַי רֹאֵי פְּנֵי הַמֶּלֶךְ הַיֹּשְׁבִים רִאשֹׁנָה בַּמַּלְכוּת: טוכְּדָת מַה־לַּעֲשׂוֹת בַּמַּלְכָּה וַשְׁתִּי עַל | אֲשֶׁר לֹא־עָשְׂתָה אֶת־מַאֲמַר הַמֶּלֶךְ אֲחַשְׁוֵרוֹשׁ בְּיַד הַסָּרִיסִים:

טזוַיֹּאמֶר מומכן כתיב מְמוּכָן לִפְנֵי הַמֶּלֶךְ וְהַשָּׂרִים לֹא עַל־הַמֶּלֶךְ לְבַדּוֹ עָוְתָה וַשְׁתִּי הַמַּלְכָּה כִּי עַל־כָּל־הַשָּׂרִים וְעַל־כָּל־הָעַמִּים אֲשֶׁר בְּכָל־מְדִינוֹת הַמֶּלֶךְ אֲחַשְׁוֵרוֹשׁ: יזכִּי־יֵצֵא דְבַר־הַמַּלְכָּה עַל־כָּל־הַנָּשִׁים לְהַבְזוֹת בַּעְלֵיהֶן בְּעֵינֵיהֶן בְּאָמְרָם הַמֶּלֶךְ אֲחַשְׁוֵרוֹשׁ אָמַר לְהָבִיא אֶת־וַשְׁתִּי הַמַּלְכָּה לְפָנָיו וְלֹא־בָאָה: יחוְהַיּוֹם הַזֶּה תֹּאמַרְנָה | שָׂרוֹת פָּרַס־וּמָדַי אֲשֶׁר שָׁמְעוּ אֶת־דְּבַר הַמַּלְכָּה לְכֹל שָׂרֵי הַמֶּלֶךְ וּכְדַי בִּזָּיוֹן וָקָצֶף: יטאִם־עַל־הַמֶּלֶךְ טוֹב יֵצֵא דְבַר־מַלְכוּת מִלְּפָנָיו וְיִכָּתֵב בְּדָתֵי פָרַס־וּמָדַי וְלֹא יַעֲבוֹר אֲשֶׁר לֹא־תָבוֹא וַשְׁתִּי לִפְנֵי הַמֶּלֶךְ אֲחַשְׁוֵרוֹשׁ וּמַלְכוּתָהּ יִתֵּן הַמֶּלֶךְ לִרְעוּתָהּ הַטּוֹבָה מִמֶּנָּה: כוְנִשְׁמַע פִּתְגָם הַמֶּלֶךְ אֲשֶׁר־יַעֲשֶׂה בְּכָל־מַלְכוּתוֹ כִּי רַבָּה הִיא וְכָל־הַנָּשִׁים יִתְּנוּ יְקָר לְבַעְלֵיהֶן לְמִגָּדוֹל וְעַד־קָטָן: כאוַיִּיטַב הַדָּבָר בְּעֵינֵי

who waited upon King Achashverosh, [11] to bring Queen Vashti before the king [wearing her] royal crown, to show the nations and the nobles her beauty, for she was [indeed] of fine appearance. [12] But Queen Vashti refused to come at the order of the king that [he had sent] through [his] attendants, and [so] the king was extremely enraged and his fury burned within him.

[13] The king then consulted the wise men, experts in astronomy, for so was the king's [practice to present every] matter before all the law and judicial experts. [14] And his close [advisers] were Karshena, Shesar, Admasa, Tarshish, Meres, Marsena and Memuchan, the seven ministers of Persia and Media who had [constant] access to the king [and] were the highest members of the realm. [15] [He consulted them as to] what, according to law, should be done with Queen Vashti, for that she did not carry out the decree of King Achashverosh [which he had sent] with his attendants.

[16] Memuchan then said before the king and the ministers, "Not only against the king did Queen Vashti act disobediently, but [also] against all the ministers and all the nations who [live] in all the states of King Achashverosh. [17] For the incident of the queen will spread among all the women [and cause them] to belittle their husbands, when [the nobles] tell [that] King Achashverosh ordered to have Queen Vashti brought before him but she did not come. [18] And [even] today, the ladies of Paras and Madai who heard about the incident of the queen will tell all the ministers of the king [about it], and this [will cause] much humiliation and anger. [19] If it pleases the king, let a royal proclamation be issued by him, and let it be inscribed among the laws of Paras and Madai and not be revoked, that Vashti would not come before King Achashverosh [and was therefore killed], and so the king will grant her royal [position] to her counterpart who is better than her. [20] The king's decree that he will enact shall then be publicized throughout his kingdom,

מגילת אסתר
Megillas Esther

וַיְהִי בִּימֵי אֲחַשְׁוֵרוֹשׁ הוּא אֲחַשְׁוֵרוֹשׁ הַמֹּלֵךְ מֵהֹדּוּ וְעַד־כּוּשׁ שֶׁבַע וְעֶשְׂרִים וּמֵאָה מְדִינָה: בַּיָּמִים הָהֵם כְּשֶׁבֶת | הַמֶּלֶךְ אֲחַשְׁוֵרוֹשׁ עַל כִּסֵּא מַלְכוּתוֹ אֲשֶׁר בְּשׁוּשַׁן הַבִּירָה: בִּשְׁנַת שָׁלוֹשׁ לְמָלְכוֹ עָשָׂה מִשְׁתֶּה לְכָל־שָׂרָיו וַעֲבָדָיו חֵיל | פָּרַס וּמָדַי הַפַּרְתְּמִים וְשָׂרֵי הַמְּדִינוֹת לְפָנָיו: בְּהַרְאֹתוֹ אֶת־עֹשֶׁר כְּבוֹד מַלְכוּתוֹ וְאֶת־יְקָר תִּפְאֶרֶת גְּדוּלָּתוֹ יָמִים רַבִּים שְׁמוֹנִים וּמְאַת יוֹם: וּבִמְלוֹאת | הַיָּמִים הָאֵלֶּה עָשָׂה הַמֶּלֶךְ לְכָל־הָעָם הַנִּמְצְאִים בְּשׁוּשַׁן הַבִּירָה לְמִגָּדוֹל וְעַד־קָטָן מִשְׁתֶּה שִׁבְעַת יָמִים בַּחֲצַר גִּנַּת בִּיתָן הַמֶּלֶךְ: חוּר | כַּרְפַּס וּתְכֵלֶת אָחוּז בְּחַבְלֵי־בוּץ וְאַרְגָּמָן עַל־גְּלִילֵי כֶסֶף וְעַמּוּדֵי שֵׁשׁ מִטּוֹת | זָהָב וָכֶסֶף עַל רִצְפַת בַּהַט־וָשֵׁשׁ וְדַר וְסֹחָרֶת: וְהַשְׁקוֹת בִּכְלֵי זָהָב וְכֵלִים מִכֵּלִים שׁוֹנִים וְיֵין מַלְכוּת רָב כְּיַד הַמֶּלֶךְ: וְהַשְּׁתִיָּה כַדָּת אֵין אֹנֵס כִּי־כֵן | יִסַּד הַמֶּלֶךְ עַל כָּל־רַב בֵּיתוֹ לַעֲשׂוֹת כִּרְצוֹן אִישׁ־וָאִישׁ:

גַּם וַשְׁתִּי הַמַּלְכָּה עָשְׂתָה מִשְׁתֵּה נָשִׁים בֵּית הַמַּלְכוּת אֲשֶׁר לַמֶּלֶךְ אֲחַשְׁוֵרוֹשׁ: בַּיּוֹם הַשְּׁבִיעִי כְּטוֹב לֵב־הַמֶּלֶךְ בַּיָּיִן אָמַר לִמְהוּמָן בִּזְּתָא חַרְבוֹנָא בִּגְתָא וַאֲבַגְתָא זֵתַר וְכַרְכַּס שִׁבְעַת הַסָּרִיסִים הַמְשָׁרְתִים אֶת־פְּנֵי הַמֶּלֶךְ אֲחַשְׁוֵרוֹשׁ: לְהָבִיא אֶת־וַשְׁתִּי הַמַּלְכָּה לִפְנֵי הַמֶּלֶךְ בְּכֶתֶר מַלְכוּת לְהַרְאוֹת הָעַמִּים

It happened in the days of Achashverosh — he is [the same] Achashverosh who was ruling over a hundred and twenty-seven states from Hodu (India) to Kush (Ethiopia): [2] At that time, when King Achashverosh had consolidated his rule over his kingdom, whose seat was in the citadel of Shushan, [3] in the third year of his reign, he made a banquet for all his ministers and servants, [with] the army of Persia and Media [and] the governors and ministers of the states [all] being present. [4] [This was] when he displayed the wealth of his royal glory and the magnificence of the majesty of his greatness. [The banquet lasted] for many days — 180 days. [5] And when these days ended, the king made a seven-day banquet for all the people located in the citadel of Shushan, from the greatest to the most insignificant, in the courtyard, garden [and] *bisan* (orchard) of the king. [6] White (*chur*), parsley-green and aquamarine (*t'cheles*) [sheets], embroidered with fine linen (*butz*) and purple [wool] (*argaman*) cords, [were spread] over silver wheels and marble pillars, [and] golden and silver couches [were set up] on a flooring of *bahat,* marble, *dar* and *sochares* [stone]. [7] And [the king ordered that the guests] be given to drink in golden vessels and [other] various kinds of vessels, and [there was] much royal wine, as [befitted] the king's wealth. [8] And [any amount of] drink was in order [since] there was no compulsion, for so the king had decreed upon every official of his household to carry out the [individual] wishes of each person.

[9] Queen Vashti also made a women's banquet at King Achashverosh's royal palace. [10] On the seventh day, when the king was merry with wine, he told Mehuman, Bizesa, Charvona, Bigsa, Avagsa, Zesar and Karkas, the seven attendants